Tom & Sherry

Tom & Sherry

How to Have It All

Elisabeth Glas

Copyright © 2015 by Elisabeth Glas

All rights reserved. No part of this book may be used or reproduced in any manner whatsoever without the written permission from the author except in the case of brief quotations embodied in critical articles or reviews. Information can be obtained through elisabethglas.com.

First edition, 2015

ISBN: 978-0-9965648-0-9 (paperback)

Cover design: Alessia Cerra

To Marta,

without whom I would not have started writing this book;

and to Reza,

without whom I would not have finished writing this book.

Contents

Opening: It used to be so easy   1

PART I. Why Tom Keeps Fighting Sherry
(and Vice Versa): The hidden forces of guilt

1. Why Guilt Matters   23
2. When What We See Is Not What It Seems   39
3. When High Performers Underperform   57
4. The Grand Delusion We All Fall For   72

PART II. What Happens When Tom and
Sherry Join Forces: The rise of a new majority

5. What We Have in Common with Smokers   95
6. What We Really Want (But Are Afraid to Ask For)   112

PART III. How Tom and Sherry Make It Happen: The power of seeing the obvious

7.	If You Want Something, Say So…	129
8.	"The Morning Routine"—An Everyday Case Example	150
9.	Learning To See the Obvious	160
	Outlook: The shape of things to come	187
	Acknowledgements	194
	Notes	195
	About the Author	211

Opening: It used to be so easy

Tom, 41, a senior partner with the management consulting firm of Szabo-Davis, sits at his desk working on his laptop when he hears a short knock at his open office door. Glancing up, he finds Sherry, 35, dressed in a dark business suit.

"Hi Tom… You have a moment?"

"That depends…" He looks her over, likes what he sees. "Sherry, right?"

She nods. "I'm only in for the day. Flew in from the Chicago Office."

"Right. The interview this morning." She nods again. "What can I do for you?"

"Nothing. Actually, I wanted to do something for you."

"All right. Well, tell me."

"This morning's debriefing following the interview with Madeline Gaines. It was disturbing."

"Excuse me?"

"Your refusal to vote was frankly unacceptable."

"Really? I thought I made myself quite clear. Beautiful women make poor executives. It's not her fault. But her looks are an unnecessary distraction. Her beauty made me biased, so I decided to abstain. Simple as that."

"That's exactly the problem, Tom. Because she is a beautiful woman, she didn't get a fair chance to receive an offer from us. No wonder we don't have more women at this firm."

"Sherry, I don't want to be rude, and you seem to be a nice and intelligent person, but I'd say you're jumping to conclusions."

"Am I? Let's look at the facts. There were two 'yes' votes against three 'no.' You, being the most senior person in the room, could have turned the decision around."

"Who says I would have voted 'yes?'"

"Nobody. All I'm saying is that your bias prevented her from getting a fair chance."

"Listen, Sherry. If the interview team would have felt strongly about her, we would have organized another interview, and perhaps she would have gotten the sixth vote you are insisting on. But nobody on the team was impressed enough to pound the table for her, not even you."

"Point taken. We both should have spoken up."

"So let me ask *you* a question, my dear."

"I'm not your dear."

"You know, you have a beautiful smile."

"Yes, I do. But it has nothing to do with your question."

"Why do you women always blame men for the situation? I do my best to recruit and promote as many women as men. But there are simply not enough qualified women. And I'm not willing to compromise on quality."

"And you shouldn't. Neither do I. But there is a reason why the recruiting and promotion pipeline for women is so thin at firms like ours."

"Really...?"

"Really. Let me tell you a story. When I decided to get pregnant, I was so sure and enthusiastic about going back to work after my maternity leave that the idea of compromising my career never even crossed my mind."

"Of course, that's what I would have expected from somebody like you."

"But while I was pregnant, I kept being asked the question: did I plan to go back to work, and if so, would it be part-time or full-time?"

"By whom? By your mother?"

"No, by pretty much everyone who saw me with my belly out to here. But that's not the point. What struck me was: nobody ever asked my husband that question, although he was earning less than I did."

"True, now that I think about it, I would *never* ask a man if he plans to stay home or work part-time once his wife has a baby. Why would I?"

Sherry's cell phone rings. Glancing down, she recognizes the number.

"Sorry, I have to take this call."

"Sure."

Sherry begins to speak into her cell phone as she steps out of Tom's office. Tom leans back in his chair, hands behind his head. A soft smile creeps up his face while trying to make sense of this unexpected exchange. Then he goes back to his laptop.

It used to be so easy. To be a good dad was to be the Breadwinner; to be a good mom was to be the Caregiver. Today, both parents want it all—to be the successful Breadwinner *and* the involved Caregiver. But it seems my grandmother was right after all when she used to say: "Elisabeth, you can't dance at two weddings." The fact is: we don't have it all, although we have tried many things.[1] We've tried to stretch the roles; we've tried to lean into each other's roles; we've even tried to flip the roles.[2] But did we ever try to get rid of the roles, simply abandon them altogether?

That's exactly what we should do if we are serious about "having it all." Let's stop dreaming. Caregivers will never fully integrate into the corporate world, and Breadwinners will never get fully involved at home, because the roles don't allow for it. Each is highly specialized—one is meant to deal with home, the other meant to deal with the workplace. And each is intended to complement the other, a kind of mutual support system. Furthermore, the roles were never meant to reflect our individual skills or preferences because who would do which role was predetermined. Traditionally, in a marriage, it went without question that the man was the breadwinner and the woman the caregiver. So it should come as no surprise that these roles offer little flexibility.

Bottom line: the concept of Breadwinner versus Caregiver is very rigid. And as long as we continue to think in terms of Breadwinners and Caregivers, we will never be able to have

OPENING: IT USED TO BE SO EASY

it all. We will never be able to fully embrace and enjoy the rich opportunities available to us today. So why then are we so attached to these roles?

"I'm sorry... That was not very polite—but the client always comes first."

Sherry reenters Tom's office with an apologizing smile. Tom looks up again from his laptop.

"No problem at all."

"I just wanted to finish my story."

"Ah, I thought you already had."

"Not really. Because what's important here is understanding why our recruiting and promotion pipeline for women is so thin."

"And what makes you think you have the answer?"

"Because after being repeatedly asked if I planned to return to work, I began to question going back or maybe only going back part-time."

"You can't be serious. Given your track record? Why would you even think that?"

"Because I was suddenly confronted by what society expects from a good mom."

"That's not true, Sherry. Today, the majority of moms work. I'm sure you know the statistics better than I do."

"Then why did everybody ask me that question?"

"No idea."

"It's because of that romanticized ideal of a loving and caring mother who would never leave her newborn child to return to work. And the more people keep asking, the more you start questioning yourself: What if my baby needs me? Am I being a bad mother? Do I even know what a baby really needs…? And unfortunately I couldn't ask the baby, himself."

"Yes, but that's just guilt."

"*Just* guilt?"

"Yes, *just* guilt. You are an intelligent woman. You can decide for yourself what you want to do, and what is best for you and your baby. Why listen to anyone else?"

"Ever heard of peer pressure? The week before I went back to work, I started receiving messages from friends and family to wish me 'good luck'—"

"What's wrong with that?"

"It wasn't what they said, but how they said it. For some reason they all felt the need to warn me—that I will feel terribly guilty for leaving the baby, but that I will eventually get over it."

"Are you serious, Sherry? That's terrible. I'd say you need a new set of friends. What do they know about how you will feel?"

"I guess they thought they were being supportive… In any case, on my first day back at work something strange happened to me: I felt guilty for not feeling guilty."

"What…? You women are crazy! If there is nothing to feel guilty about, you invent something."

"Please, Tom."

"Sorry, but I have no patience for things like that. If what you're suggesting is true, then I can't help with the pipeline problem."

"You never feel guilty… ever?"

OPENING: IT USED TO BE SO EASY

"No. I mean I feel bad when I haven't reached out to my parents for a while, but I don't feel guilty for anything. I'm proud of my career. I earned it. And I'm proud of my kids. Have I made mistakes? Of course, who hasn't? But nothing to feel guilty about."

"How many kids do you have?"

"Three."

"That's nice. Your wife is taking care of them?"

Tom hesitates, trying to decide how to answer her. At last: "We're divorced, but yes. She has custody and I support them. In any case, I always did what I felt was right."

"I'm sure you did. But I'm also sure you feel guilty sometimes, you just don't admit it... Or let me give you the benefit of the doubt: You don't realize it."

"Thank you, Sherry, that's generous of you. But believe me, I do *not* feel guilty. I make conscious decisions and then I stick to them. I decided to have this career. I knew what I was getting into, and I accept the consequences. Period."

"So you consciously put your kids second?"

"No. I wouldn't call it second, but that's just how we divided the workload: I'm the breadwinner, and she takes care of the kids."

"You never miss your kids?"

"Of course I do, like everybody else. But it's simply not possible to combine both with a demanding career like ours."

She looks at him for a long moment without speaking, then adds:

"Well, I do. At least I try."

"You must be a genius!"

OPENING: IT USED TO BE SO EASY

"Thank you, but no. I'm just not willing to compromise on what really matters. In fact, it is possible to combine both, but men too often just don't try."

"How can you say that?"

"Because it's true. What man would ever dare to put his kids before his job, or at least on par with it?"

"Now there is a bold statement."

"Think about it."

"I will... believe me, I will."

For a brief moment they look at each other in silence. Then Sherry smiles:

"I know you will. But I have to go or I'll miss my plane."

"Sure... and thank you, Sherry. I always appreciate it when people make me think, and this afternoon, you certainly did. Make sure you drop by next time you visit our office."

"Thanks, I will."

"I'll look forward to it. Take care."

"You, too. Bye."

Sherry checks her messages while leaving Tom's office. Tom watches her walking out. Then he looks her up in the online directory of the firm and saves her cell phone number in his.

Why are we so attached to the roles of Breadwinners and Caregivers, roles that rigidly constrain the way we spend our time? They might have made sense in the immediate post-war years, when men were still better educated than women and hence were predestined to be breadwinners.[3] But that's no longer the case.[4] Then why don't we spend time the way

OPENING: IT USED TO BE SO EASY

we want, each family in its own way, the way that suits them best?

To answer this, we need to take a closer look at how we actually spend our time. Given that every day is limited to 24 hours, spending more time on one activity means spending less on another. Back in the 1960s, when moms started entering the workforce and spending more time on paid work, they had to spend less on something else. And that something else had to either be picked up by somebody else, or they had to give up a third activity for it, or they had to let go of it completely. And then of course, the same was true for the other side of the equation, dad. If he wanted to pick up activities from mom, then he had to spend less time on something else. Understanding how parents decided to spend their time since then, should give us a clue as to why we continue to insist on the roles of Breadwinners and Caregivers.

Ladies first: Nationwide time-use studies covering the period from 1965 to 2008 show that the weekly hours mothers spent on paid work has increased dramatically since 1965.[5] This has resulted in fewer hours spent on housework, a phenomenon supported by technology and a variety of timesaving innovations.[6] However, it did not impact the time they spent on childcare. On the contrary, the weekly hours mom spent with her kids increased in parallel. This is true for both stay-at-home and working moms. In fact, a working mother in 2008 spent as much time with her kids as a stay-at-home mom did in 1965. As mom had already traded the hours she used to spend doing housework for paid work, it left her only one category of time in which to find these extra hours to spend with her kids: Her private time.[7] And that's exactly what she did. She tapped into her own time to spend more hours with her children.

Now why would mom do this, especially if we consider that over the same time period dad increased his time with the kids as well?[8] In fact, if we combine the additional hours spent by dad with the extra hours devoted by mom, parents in 2008 spent nine more hours per week on childcare than their peers of forty years ago.

The answer is simple: Mom feels guilty, guilty for not spending enough time with her children.[9] Having been raised and continuing to live in an environment clearly divided into Breadwinners and Caregivers, deep in their hearts women still believe that it is a mother's role to be the primary caregiver. This doesn't preclude her from having a career, but her career comes second. This belief is re-enforced daily by pretty much everyone around them, their spouse, their parents and parents-in-law, their mommy friends, their boss, their colleagues at work, everyone. So it should come as no surprise that moms increased the time spent with their kids to protect their traditional role as the exclusive caregiver.

Now let's look at dad. We have already learned that between 1965 and 2008 dad gradually increased his time with the kids.[10] He also picked up a few hours of housework from mom. To compensate, he was forced to reduce his hours spent on paid work. Over time however, in parallel with further increasing his time with the kids (as housework began to level off), he once again began to increase his time at work.

OPENING: IT USED TO BE SO EASY

As dad had already traded the hours he used to spend on paid work for hours he now spends on childcare and housework, he had only one category of time left to find these extra hours for paid work: His private time. And that's exactly what he did. He tapped into his own time to spend more time at work.

Why would dad increase his workload just as mom's contribution to the household income began to significantly increase? In 1960, only 25% of married couples with kids were two income families. By 2011, the number of married couples with kids and two incomes had more than doubled to 60%.[11] Given this substantial increase in mom's contribution to the family income, why would dad not decide to relax, at least a little bit?

The answer is the same as what we saw with mom: Dad feels guilty, guilty for not spending enough time on the job nurturing his career. Having been raised and continuing to live in an environment clearly divided into Breadwinners and Caregivers, deep in his heart dad still believes he is meant to be the primary breadwinner. This doesn't mean he wants to spend less time with his kids, but family comes second. This belief is enforced daily by pretty much everyone around him, his spouse, his parents and parents-in-law, his buddies, his boss, his colleagues at work, everyone. So it should come as no surprise that dads unconsciously protect their traditional role as the exclusive breadwinner.

Obviously there are many factors influencing how we spend our time. But the trend here is important, and the trend could not be more clear: Confronted with perceived threats to their traditional roles, both parents make explicit efforts to preserve their respective roles as Breadwinner and Caregiver, as if they have a secret pact to maintain the status quo. But there is no secret pact. It is simply our own guilt that keeps us from breaking with the past.

"Look who is back!"

Spotting Sherry at one of the coffee machines in the office cafeteria, Tom gives her a smile. Having taken off his jacket and tie earlier in the day, he is in the process of rolling up his sleeves. Despite being clearly impressed by his trim, athletic body, Sherry tries not to show it:

"Oh, hi Tom! Good to see you."

"The pleasure's mine. How have you been?"

He pours himself a cup of coffee as well.

"Good, good. How about yourself? Could you please pass me the milk?"

"Sure, here you go. I'm fine, thanks. When did you get in?"

"This morning. I caught the early flight out of O'Hare."

Stirring his coffee, he teases her.

"Well, that's a relief. I'd hate to think you'd forgotten your promise."

"Which promise?"

"To stop by my office next time you're here."

Flattered, she smiles while downplaying his invitation.

"Really? I didn't realize you were expecting me."

"So what brings you here anyway?"

"The 'WomenAspire' workshop."

"The *what* workshop?"

"'WomenAspire.' It's a two-day seminar for female

OPENING: IT USED TO BE SO EASY

Associates from offices all across the country to discuss creative solutions for combining work and family."

"I see. So you are working on the famous pipeline!"

"Actually, I guess I am."

"You guess...? So you're not sure? Maybe it's the name. Instead of 'WomenAspire,' how about 'Fifty Ways to Fight Guilt?'"

"Tom, please. But at least you were listening last time."

"I told you, I always pay attention when someone says something worth listening to. But this workshop, you sound like you have reservations."

"Not really. There's nothing wrong with the workshop, if it were open to everybody. Unfortunately, it isn't."

"How come?"

"Men are not invited."

"You sound surprised. Why should men be invited? I can't imagine many men being interested in the topic."

"I completely disagree, Tom. Can you imagine how many men are tired of continuously justifying their long work hours at home, of getting those nasty looks every time they miss dinner with the kids?"

Tom reacts with a knowing smile, rolling his eyes.

"Sounds like you've been talking to my ex-wife. I know those looks too well... And I do not appreciate them at all... They suggest that I purposely miss dinner with the kids, which is absurd."

"So?"

"So what, Sherry?"

"Wouldn't those men—you, for instance—be interested in

knowing how to change this? ... And forget about guilt for a moment."

Trapped by his own logic, Tom shakes his head while conceding the point.

"Thank you, counselor. Of course I would be interested."

"Then you should participate in the workshop, Tom... But of course, you can't because you're not even invited!"

"I'm not sure I follow."

"Ok, let me try again: The workshop is about how to combine work and family. Being home in time for dinner with the kids has everything to do with combining work and family. Would you agree so far?"

"Yes."

"Then the logical consequence would be to invite everybody who is interested in how to combine work and family."

"True."

"But we don't. By inviting only women we are implying that it's acceptable for women to combine both, but not for men."

"That's just the reality, Sherry."

"No. It's how we *want* it to be, not how it *has* to be. And as long as we keep those workshops exclusively for women, nothing will change—on the contrary, we are actually reinforcing the traditional roles."

"Now you've completely lost me. How can these workshops reinforce the traditional roles? Aren't they supposed to be doing just the opposite?"

"Of course. But think about the message these workshops

are sending. What they're saying to women is: We have organized this workshop for you, dear women, because we assume that you will be the primary caregiver and don't want you to feel guilty about it, despite having a career."

"Got it. And what's the message to the men?"

"We don't invite you to this workshop, dear men, because we assume that you will be the primary breadwinner, and we don't want you to feel guilty about it, despite having kids."

Clearly, from the look in his eye, Tom is impressed by Sherry's arguments. He holds up both hands in mock surrender.

"Very impressive. You've convinced me, Sherry, you really have… I actually like the way you reason. Basically what you are saying is that with such workshops we are simply reinforcing the stereotypes. And I agree. But why then do you participate in the workshops at all?"

"Good question, Tom… I don't know. I guess because it is expected."

"Maybe you should reconsider. Think about it. By participating, you're actually supporting something you don't believe in." Checking his watch, he realizes the time. "I have to go. Have fun at the workshop."

Tom walks out of the cafeteria, greeting several colleagues in the hallway. Sherry pauses for a moment, mulling over what Tom's just said. Then taking her coffee with her, she turns and exits in the opposite direction.

Sticking to the traditional roles doesn't mean that we are prevented from venturing outside of these roles. In fact, most of us want and do so. But we do so *on top* of our pre-assigned roles, not instead of them. As a result, we end up with caregivers who add breadwinner-tasks on top of their traditional workloads, and breadwinners who add caregiver-tasks on top of their respective workloads. This behavior of continuously adding tasks as we search for personal satisfaction is neither fulfilling nor smart. Not for women, not for men.

What makes this unfulfilling is our lack of a true choice as to how we spend our time. Let's not fool ourselves. The overarching goal when choosing how to spend our time is not maximizing our personal fulfillment, but minimizing our guilt. To do so we always prioritize pre-assigned tasks over add-on tasks, independent of our individual skills and qualifications, and independent of our personal preferences and needs. That's why caregivers who decide to go back to work (their add-on task) frequently prefer to work part-time or choose a less demanding career path. And that's why breadwinners who decide to get involved with their kids (their add-on task) generally prefer to participate in single events rather than commit to regular ongoing activities.[12]

It is also an extremely poor use of our time. Guilt drives mom to do the caregiver-tasks, independent of what dad decides to do. And guilt drives dad to do the breadwinner-tasks, independent of what mom decides to do. As a result, by duplicating our efforts we squander our most precious commodity—time—without even realizing it. Even worse, we start competing for tasks instead of complementing each other. What other explanation is there for parents adding

OPENING: IT USED TO BE SO EASY

nine additional hours per week—the equivalent of a full workday—to the time spent with their kids? And how else is it possible to explain why working long hours has become a symbol for success instead of inefficiency?

So here we are, endlessly debating how to have it all without understanding the root cause of our behavior, without realizing that both men and women are actually working against their own best interests, and while doing so, wasting precious time. There *must* be a better way. Here are the three fundamental things we need to get straight if we want to have it all:

First, this is not a gender problem. Girls have the opportunity to study and succeed the same as boys, and men can leverage the same flexibility offered at work as women, but far too often they don't. We do have a choice, but we don't exercise it. And the reason is guilt. It is guilt that causes us to comply with the standard roles, the roles of the male breadwinner and the female caregiver. It is guilt that artificially limits our choices. But guilt is subversive because it influences our behavior and decisions without us even realizing it. And as a result, we keep solving for the wrong problem.

Second, running a household is not a zero sum game in which the breadwinner's success comes at the caregiver's expense and vice versa. On the contrary, men and women are in this together. But because we mistake it for a gender problem, we fight an enemy that doesn't exist.

Third, having it all is not a question of having enough time but of how to make best use of the time we have. Instead of allowing others to dictate how we allocate our time, we should start using time the way we want, respecting our true preferences and leveraging the best skills each parent has to offer—independent of his or her gender. Then, and only then, will we be able to free up the time that is currently wasted by managing guilt and ultimately give us enough time to have it all.

This book is divided into three parts: Part One is devoted to diagnosis and explores the hidden forces of guilt. We will learn how guilt works, what tricks it plays on us and how it got us to where we are today. Part Two offers solutions as well as a pathway out. We will learn with whom to work, with what kind of attitude, and which dynamics can be leveraged to pave the way for having it all. Part Three focuses on implementation and will teach us the day-to-day implications for each of us. We will learn to spot wasted time, how to avoid it, and where to reallocate that time in order to make having it all a reality.

Let me add a personal note: The worst review I could possibly imagine for this book is someone saying that it is "well-researched." This book is not about providing yet another collection of eye-opening facts. We all know the facts by now. This book is about making a simple, but crucial point and providing a pragmatic solution. It offers a unique perspective by completely reframing the problem that we are trying to solve. So if you are hoping for catchy facts to dish up at your next cocktail party, stop reading. If you are looking for a solution, buckle up.

PART 1

Why Tom Keeps Fighting
Sherry (and Vice Versa):
The hidden forces of guilt

1

Why Guilt Matters

Although it's just past noon and her assistant has gone to lunch, Sherry is still at her computer, picking at the salad she purchased from the young woman working for Moveable Feast earlier this morning. As she carefully goes over the file she's been working on, the ring tone from her cell phone tells her she has a message. Pleased to see it's from Tom, she touches the screen:

"Hi Sherry, this is Tom. You'll be in my class tomorrow. Looking forward to seeing you."

Smiling, she touches the message bar and texts back:

"Hi Tom. Your class? I thought it was just for newly elected partners like me."

"Actually, I'll be your instructor. Jack Squires was supposed to do it, but he's had a family emergency and asked me to step in."

"Sorry to hear about Jack. So I guess I'll see you tomorrow then!"

"BTW: I've been thinking about your question—about if I put my kids second."

"And?"

"I don't. I've always been there when they needed me."

"Good for you."

"E.g., when my wife was in hospital for six months, I was there. I ran the household."

"You stopped working?"

"Of course not. I organized myself differently. Everybody in the office was very supportive."

"I'm sure they were. What happened then?"

"What you mean by 'then'…?"

"After your wife came home."

"I went back to my regular routine."

"Why?"

"Why not, Sherry?"

"Because you had found a way to combine both. Why not continue to do so?"

"It was a special situation, so I stepped in. Once she recovered, I went back to normal."

"B.S. You didn't dare to continue. You felt guilty about not spending more time at work."

"You know my opinion on guilt."

"Opinion is the wrong word. Try ignorance."

"Boy, you really know how to hurt a guy."

"What did you expect? Applause?"

"I don't expect anything from you, Sherry. When will you be flying in?"

"Tomorrow morning."

"Can I offer you a ride? La Guardia Airport is on my way."

"Sure. Why not."

"Will be my pleasure, assuming you're in a better mood. Send your flight details to my assistant, please."

"Will do. I have to run now. Got to finish this file by 4 so that I can take my son to the park. See you tomorrow."

Ending the SMS thread, Tom is satisfied with the execution of his idea and starts planning what to pack for the two days ahead. He wants to look sharp.

Sherry will pack tomorrow morning. Right now there's a more pressing matter: Pick up her son and decide which ice cream truck they might stop at.

We all know how guilt feels. Some of us experience it more often, others less. But what many of us don't know—or significantly underestimate—is how guilt impacts us, how guilt influences the way we behave and the choices we make. In fact, it is critical to understand how guilt infiltrates our daily decision making process without us even noticing it. So if we are serious about having it all, we need to learn how guilt works and what tricks it plays on us.

Obviously, understanding guilt in its full complexity is an endeavor that goes well beyond the scope of this book. But there are three things we need to know about guilt:[1]

First, the fact *that* we feel guilty is something natural, something we are all born with, without exception. Some of us might be more prone to guilt than others, but we are all vulnerable to its effects.

Second, *what* we feel guilty about is man-made. It is defined by the context of our lives, our family, our workplace, our society. And since we define it, we also have the power to change it.

Third, the subversive thing about guilt is how it impacts our behavior and decision-making without us realizing it. It is therefore crucial that we understand precisely how and when guilt influences us.

Let's start with point one: The capacity to feel guilty has been hard-wired into our brains as part of our evolutionary make-up. Think of guilt as a moral control mechanism that humans evolved over thousands of years in their competition for survival, the survival of the fittest. Being the fittest is not just about the physical fitness of each individual, it's about reproduction. The fittest were the ones who had the highest reproduction rate, not in absolute terms, but relative to their competition. So it wasn't good enough to just reproduce. They also had to make sure that their offspring survive, and then reproduce in turn—ultimately growing into a little community.[2]

How did they make it possible for their offspring to survive? It was necessary to provide food and shelter, of course; but it was equally essential to control the natural instinct for survival at any cost. For example, one such cost might have be the killing of their siblings or other group members in the quest for primacy. How do they tame these instincts? Through the development of the capacity to feel guilt. Let me explain: Imagine you and I are members of the same group or tribe and we are hungry. You finally find an edible fruit. Unfortunately, it is hanging too high for you to reach. But you can reach it with my help. Of course, to secure my cooperation you will need to share your fruit with me, otherwise you will feel guilty. But next time I find a fruit, I will share it with you, otherwise I feel guilty. Hence, the probability for both of us to survive is substantially increased through our mutual capacity to feel guilty. Without that capacity, we both might have starved or at least gone hungry.[3]

As small family units grew into communities and eventually societies, the importance of guilt as a moral control mechanism became even more important (e.g. if you and I agree on a deal and you break it, you feel guilty. Or if I ask you to do something illegal or immoral, you will not just blindly execute my request. Rather you will refrain from doing it, otherwise you will feel guilty).

For a moment, imagine a world unrestrained by guilt. Would you want to live in such a world? I wouldn't. Of course, you will always find people with bad intentions, but that's what we have laws for. So in its purest function, guilt can be a force for good, like a friendly reminder to behave, which long-term will benefit all members of a society.

"Good morning!"

Waving his arms, Tom gets out of his car when he sees Sherry approaching. He takes her luggage and puts it into the trunk. He is dressed casually today, but with the same attention to detail as always. Sherry lets herself glide into the leather passenger seat, suppressing a yawn. It's early but she's already been up for several hours. She is glad she chose to wear her comfy skinny pants and sneakers.

"Good early morning."

"If you don't mind me saying, you look in desperate need of coffee."

"I absolutely am."

"Good, I know just the spot, and it's right on our way."

Turning the key, Tom slips the car into gear, and they drive off. At first, neither speaks, then Tom breaks the ice.

"So how was the stroll in the park with your son yesterday?"

"Nice, nothing spectacular. But of course, he is very sweet… I really enjoy these little moments with him a lot."

"How old is he?"

"Four…" Looking up, she reacts. "Shouldn't we have taken that last exit?"

"Excuse me?"

"That last exit. I think we should have taken it. We have to go north."

"Am I driving or are you?"

Sensing a sudden edge in Tom's voice, Sherry backs off.

"Sorry, just trying to be helpful. I hate to be late, especially the first day. And I'm pretty sure we have to go north."

"Thank you, Sherry, I know what I'm doing."

"Good."

"Yes, good."

As the silence between them lengthens, Tom activates the

GPS to satisfy her concerns. Instantly, the GPS starts recalculating the route as the female voice suggests they take the next exit and turn around. Annoyed, Tom follows the instructions without saying a word, then flashes a boyish, self-conscious smile.

"Sounds like she agrees with you."

Spontaneously, both share a laugh.

"What can I say, Sherry!"

"You don't have to say anything."

"Come on, I know exactly what you are thinking right now."

"Really? What am I thinking?"

"Something like: Another chauvinist knuckle-dragger who refuses to take directions from a woman."

"Close. Except that I wouldn't have called you a 'knuckle-dragger.'"

"Very generous of you. Anyway, if you pay close attention, I'm sure you will figure out how I reason."

"I'm sure I will."

"Can we switch topics?"

"Anytime."

Tom and Sherry drive silently as Tom considers a different approach.

"You know, even if you look at it from an evolutionary perspective, since the Stone Age men were the ones out hunting. Which is why they needed to develop a strong sense of direction to find their way back to the cave."

Sherry has to suppress a smile.

"I'm sure you're right. But that still doesn't say anything about a woman's sense of direction."

"True."

"And if your reasoning is correct, then—for example—women should be better cooks, because that's what they've had to do every day since humans climbed down from the trees."

"Well, they are, at least the ones I know. My mom, my ex-wife, my ex-mother-in-law, they are all fantastic cooks."

"And I suppose Wolfgang Puck wears a dress."

Tom laughs in spite of himself as Sherry finesses his obvious over-generalization. Pleased that he liked her joke, Sherry continues.

"The truth is, all the world's top chefs are male, or at least the vast majority are." Then with a small smile, she adds, "Of course, they all learned from their mothers."

Tom laughs again.

"Okay, okay, I get it."

"Really, Tom, stereotypes have not much to do with reality. They are just convenient. We create them to make our lives easier, not better."

"How? Care to explain?"

"They give us structure, help us to categorize people, behaviors, any number of things. With stereotypes in place we have to think less."

"I can feel it. Here comes another bold statement!"

"My specialty."

"Quick question: You still need that cup of coffee?"

"Are you kidding? Of course, I need my coffee."

WHY GUILT MATTERS

Tom takes the next exit and parks in front of a rundown building. Sherry sees the coffee shop sign only at second glance. Tom realizes her surprise:

"Trust me, Sherry, I've been here before. And—if I'm informed correctly—choosing coffee is a guilt-free and gender-neutral activity, so you should be fine."

"Am I that bad?"

"Not always," he teases. "What can I bring you?"

"Latte, please."

Tom gets out of the car and walks over to the coffee shop. Sherry follows him with her eyes. This time she doesn't suppress the smile.

The second thing we need to know about guilt is that the source of what makes us feel guilty is man-made. Guilt is a question of perception. We feel guilty every time we perceive ourselves going against a moral standard. Standards, however, are not given; standards are made. Every society, every company, every family defines its own moral standards. So depending on which society we live in, which company we work for, and which family we are part of, we might feel guilty for a completely different set of reasons. Now if every society, every company, every family can define their own standards, then it follows that they can also change those standards. And thus guilt must be seen as a product of our own design.[4]

Of course, standards don't change overnight. But they can change, and they do change. Let's take a simple example: smoking. There was a time—and not so long ago—when smoking was considered to be cool, when society's heroes and heroines were smokers. It wouldn't have crossed any smoker's mind to feel strange or even guilty to light a cigarette on the train, in a bar, you name it. Now look at society today. Smoking is not only considered unhealthy for those who smoke, but it's perceived as a public offense to the rest of the society as well. As this example demonstrates, and we will look at it in more detail in Part Two of this book, we are, indeed, very capable of successfully changing standards. And by changing a standard I don't mean to marginally adjust it, I mean to turn it upside down.

The key to success is how we frame the problem, because any given standard only holds as long as it is supported by the majority—be it the majority of a society, of a company, or of a family. Once this is no longer the case, the standard looses its power to induce guilt. Take a moment and think of the instances when you feel guilty: You only feel guilty if the majority of people around you perceive you as being at odds with an accepted standard. If a minority perceives you as being at odds with that same standard, you couldn't care less. Hence, in order to establish a new standard we have to turn the existing majority into a minority. Put another way, we have to replace the existing majority with a new one. And to do this, we need to frame the problem in such a way that allows us to attract the support of enough people to create a new majority.

"Let's have a drink. I can't let you go sleep like this."

Tom holds the entry door of the hotel for Sherry and

guides her in the direction of the bar. Sherry is extremely upset and has a hard time keeping her voice low:

"How dare he ask me if I'm the assistant…?!"

"It caught me by surprise, too. I can't remember the last time I experienced such thoughtless prejudice."

"Then why didn't you say anything?"

"To be honest, I was more amused than surprised. I wanted to see how you'd handle it."

"How I'd handle it? You must be kidding me! What is this, a Boy's Club?"

"Sherry, you don't need to yell at me. Lower your voice."

"Sorry, you're right. I apologize. I don't mean to take it out on you. But why do men automatically assume a woman is an assistant? How about asking if I'm a partner?"

"He could. But if you are not, wouldn't that be equally embarrassing for you?"

"Tom, we are attending a partner training session. So how high is the probability that I'm *not* a partner? Believe me, if I would have been male, the assumption would have been the other way around."

"You can't know that for sure, but I agree. There are barely any male assistants, so the probability is low if you were a man that you would be one. Pure statistics, Sherry."

"Please, Tom. There are many ways to test the water before making simple assumptions based on statistics."

"Like what?"

"Like asking where I studied? Might give you a good first indicator."

"Sure. But then life starts getting complicated. And I'm not a big proponent of political correctness."

"This has nothing to do with political correctness. This is simply rude."

"I know you are angry, Sherry. And you have a right to be. But you need to calm down. What would you like to drink?"

"I'll take a cognac."

"Good choice. Will do you good." He nods to the bartender. "Make it two."

"And you have to admit, Tom, that I did remain polite, at least at the beginning."

"Yes, you did."

"But once he assumed I would be working part-time because I have a child, I really couldn't take it any longer."

"But you do work part-time, don't you?"

"Hell, yes."

"So what's the problem?"

"The problem is that I was almost relieved that I was able to answer with a 'yes.'"

"How come?"

"Because it makes me feel like less of a terrible mom."

"Sherry, please, what has that got to do with this?"

"Guilt."

"Oh no, no… Not again!"

The cognac is served. Tom picks up his glass and raises it as if to toast, but Sherry avoids his eyes. She doesn't want to share her emotions.

"Sherry, did I say something? I'm sorry, I didn't mean to…"

"It's okay. It's not you. It just feels like I'm caught in an endless loop of feeling guilty with no solution in sight."

"Come on. You are doing great! You have a fantastic son, I assume a supportive husband, and recently got elected partner—what solution are you looking for?"

For a prolonged moment, she says nothing, then:

"Actually, I'm divorced."

Caught flat-footed, Tom attempts to mask his surprise.

"I'm sorry to hear it."

"Nothing to be sorry about. It was my choice. But that's not the point. The point is that everybody behaves as if there is a right and a wrong way of doing things, but there isn't... or maybe there is?"

"What things do you mean, Sherry?"

"Things like going part-time. There is this expectation out there that moms have to work part-time, or at least work fewer hours than men—that they can't handle a full workload and a child, too."

"Now let me ask you a question, Sherry: Did *you* decide to go part-time—as you call it? Or did you let the *others* decide for you that you had to go part-time?"

"What sort of a question is that, Tom? Of course *I* decided."

"Are you sure? Because from here, it doesn't sound like that's the choice you would have preferred."

His words cause her to hesitate and reconsider.

"To be honest, I don't know... At the time, I thought I did. And trust me, it was a tough negotiation to get what I wanted. But now, I just don't know. I guess I'm not as completely immune to those kinds of expectations as I always thought I was."

"That's okay, Sherry. That's perfectly okay indeed."

"I'm just tired. Very tired. I need to go to bed now."

"You should. I still have some work, but let me walk you to the elevators."

"No worries, I'll find my way. Good night, Tom… Thanks for letting me blow off some steam. I'll be fine in the morning. Good night."

"Night." He watches her move out of the bar and across the lobby to the elevators, more intrigued than before.

The third thing we need to learn about guilt is the way it distorts our perceptions and how it can influence both our behavior and decision-making. Ultimately, we need to be able to differentiate which of our behaviors and decisions reflect our true preferences and which are driven by guilt. Only then we will be able to regain full control over them.[5]

The most diabolical thing about guilt is its self-fulfilling dynamic. This is how it works: The more we feel guilty about deviating from the standard roles of Breadwinner and Caregiver, the harder we try to adhere to what is expected of us in order to minimize our guilt. And the more we comply with these roles, the more we reinforce them, making us feel even guiltier next time we deviate from them.

There are two mechanisms by which guilt keeps us trapped in this vicious cycle: Number one: Guilt narrows our perception of what is possible. Every time we have to make a choice, our brain automatically excludes all options that trigger guilt or at least makes them appear less desirable. This makes the solution space appear much smaller than it actually is. And it makes the constraints surrounding it look much more intimidating than they actually are. As a result, there is a high probability that we will end up making another guilt-driven choice, but perceive it as our true choice simply because our guilt makes the constraints look real.

Number two: Guilt lowers our self-esteem. Feeling continuously guilty about what we do challenges the natural trust we have in ourselves to assess what is best for us. As a result, we underperform. Guilt-driven underperformance shows itself in two ways. We either start to over-deliver, to put in extra effort and go the extra mile in order to compensate for what we feel guilty about, or we start holding ourselves back and downplay the importance of what we are feeling guilty about.

There is one more thing we need to understand about guilt: Some of us, in particular men, might argue that rather than guilt, it is shame that they are experiencing. While scientists disagree on exactly where guilt stops and shame begins, a helpful way to think about it is that deviating from a standard makes us feel guilty, not living up to a standard makes us feel ashamed. In other words, guilt is triggered by wrongdoing, shame by shortcomings. But in daily life, it's hard to tell them apart.[6]

However, since they are both a reaction to how others feel about us—or how we believe they feel about us—for the purposes of this book, we will consider them to be identical.

Both of them influence our behavior and choices in a similar way. Feeling ashamed instead of guilty for leaving work early to pick up our child doesn't really make a big difference since we feel bad either way.

2

When What We See Is Not What It Seems

"Wasn't that bad after all, was it?"

Tom and Sherry are on their way back to La Guardia Airport. Sherry hesitates as she mentally reviews the training before answering:

"Compared to what...?" She asks at last with a small smile. "Getting lost on the highway?"

Enjoying her sense of humor, Tom laughs.

"No, actually it wasn't bad at all. But to be honest, I didn't learn that much new. It was more about meeting the other partners and getting a better sense of the firm, which, I admit, was very nice."

"That's the main purpose of the training anyway... We probably shouldn't call it 'training.' But our firm likes to make everything sound like work."

"That is very true."

"In any case, I've been meaning to ask you, how was your 'WomenAspire' workshop the other day?"

"Uneventful, or at least that's my view. How to manage travel, how to manage the predictability of your workload, how to find a mentor, how to plan maternity leave—all the usual suspects."

Tom nods, "Interesting."

"Really…? How is this interesting?"

"Because with the exception of maternity leave, those are the same topics I discuss at workshops with associates, independent of gender."

"That's exactly what I tried to tell you when we met in the cafeteria the other day."

"I know, I know, Sherry. I'm learning. Just give me time. You have been thinking about this for quite a while, to me it is completely new."

"I realize that. I guess I just have a hard time accepting it—it feels so obvious to me… For example, why don't you guys discuss maternity leave? Give me one good reason—"

Seeing Tom struggling, she answers for him.

"Because you don't perceive it as an option… Because you exclude it right from the get-go."

Weighing her words, he nods, "Could well be."

"And the women do exactly the same thing."

"What do you mean?"

"Most women exclude the idea of maternity leave for men right from the get-go, too. Guess what the women at the workshop the other day told me when I asked them why there were no men in the room?"

"No idea."

"They said: Because men are not interested in the topic."

"And you said: No, because they were not invited."

"Exactly! But you know what really drives me crazy? Too many women don't seem to get it. Everybody just goes with the flow."

"Ever think that maybe they really don't want a change? As a women, if you don't get promoted you can always blame the system—nothing like having a convenient excuse."

"Come on, Tom. These are some of the most ambitious women in the country. They don't fool themselves like that."

"I wouldn't be so sure. What's your take on why they just accept things as they are? And don't say guilt. I will not accept that for an answer."

Sherry smiles at his response.

"Maybe I have finally found somebody who gets my point."

"I'm glad you're realizing I'm on your side. It's taken you a while."

"Well, it was not obvious. First, you are a man. Second, you look like the traditional model."

Tom pauses for a second, then with a boyish smile he asks: "Have I just caught you being trapped in stereotypes yourself, my dear?"

Sherry hesitates, then nods with a smile: "I guess you did… Again."

Sherry leans back into the passenger seat and looks at Tom, impressed with his openness:

"I'm glad we decided to go together."

"Me too... mind if we put on some music?"

"Not at all. What do you usually listen to?"

Reaching over, he turns on the radio. "Actually, my tastes are pretty eclectic. Why don't you decide..."

As Sherry begins to search for a radio station, they drive on.

When we feel overwhelmed or frustrated with a situation, it's very tempting to blame everything and everyone around us. And it's very hard to turn the mirror back on ourselves and see what *we* could be doing differently. But what if there is nothing to blame?

That's exactly where we are today. Don't get me wrong. I'm obviously not suggesting that we have it all. It's not the result that matters. What matters is how we get there. I'm talking about the fact that there are not many formal constraints left for us to blame or eliminate. Our predecessors have done a tremendous job over the past several decades getting rid of them. The only thing missing is for us parents to step up and make use of the full set of options already out there.

Then why don't we do so? Because we don't always see them. Let me be precise: We don't *want* to see them. In any given situation, there are choices to be made. However, while we are well aware of the options, we don't consider all of them to be real. In fact, for every decision we make, we unconsciously create two categories of options: The real ones (the ones we perceive to be within reach) and the unreal ones (the ones we perceive to be out of reach). We then mentally eliminate all the unreal options and pick one of the real ones.

WHEN WHAT WE SEE IS NOT WHAT IT SEEMS

At the end of the process, we feel content with our choice given the circumstances.

However, what looks like a compromise between what we want and what is possible is, in reality, a trade-off between how much guilt we are willing to bear and how many concessions we are willing to make. In other words, which is more painful: Going against the standard practice and feeling guilty or giving up something precious and feeling unsatisfied? Looking at our current behavior, it seems that we perceive guilt to be far more painful than the lack of personal satisfaction.[1]

Surprised? Let's go back to the decision-making process and try to understand what happens. When we divide our options into the two categories, real versus unreal, we try to anticipate how much guilt each option will create versus how much personal satisfaction we will give up. Think of it as your personal guilt/satisfaction scale on which each option is ranked from 1 to 10. A ranking of "1" means zero guilt, but limited personal satisfaction. A ranking of "10" stands for maximum guilt, but full personal satisfaction.

On this scale, the quintessential Breadwinner feels exceptionally guilty for every minute he doesn't spend on work during the week. Hence, his willingness to give up quality time with his wife and kids as required by his job—at least during the week—is very high. This is the type of Breadwinner you would see showing up for the last five minutes of his son's birthday party, as a reflection of the maximum guilt he is willing to accept. The more moderate Breadwinner will feel less guilty for spending time on other things than work during the week and consequently insists on a minimum of quality time with his wife and kids in order to be satisfied. This type of Breadwinner you would see dropping off or picking up the kids at school on a regular basis and you would see him participating in their child's doctor's appointment without covering it up as a business meeting.

Equally, the quintessential Caregiver feels maximum guilt for every minute she doesn't spend with or for her kids. Hence her willingness to give up any sort of satisfaction or recognition from a promising career remains high. This is the type of Caregiver you would see heavily involved in all sorts of volunteer work related to her kids reflecting the maximum amount of guilt she is prepared to shoulder (the total number of hours spent volunteering can easily equal that of a paid part-time, if not full-time, job, work that is perfectly acceptable provided it is child-related).[2] The more moderate Caregiver, on the other hand, will feel less guilty for spending time on things other than her kids and hence insists upon at least some sort of a paid career outside the home in order to be satisfied. This is the type of Caregiver you would find working in a meaningful job, having negotiated a work schedule that suits her needs.

Of course, each of us has his or her own personal guilt/satisfaction scale. In fact, each is unique and therefore they are not meant to be comparable. The sole purpose of creating such a scale is to turn us into conscious decision makers. Here is how:

First, the scale creates awareness. It basically puts a price tag

WHEN WHAT WE SEE IS NOT WHAT IT SEEMS

on each decision: "If I decide to do A, what will I be giving up? And how much worth is it to me?"

Second, being aware of the price of each decision will help us to know where to draw the line, to identify the point beyond which we are no longer willing to go. Unless we recognize the cost of our decisions, we run the risk of stacking one guilt-driven decision upon another without realizing it until we are virtually overwhelmed.

Third (and most importantly), knowing the cost of each decision will encourage us to explore options that we might previously have considered but discarded as unrealistic. This re-evaluation of what is possible will help us to identify and overcome the many false constraints that we have developed in an attempt to minimize our guilt.

"Knock, knock, Happy Sunday! May I…?"

Without realizing it, Tom inadvertently hit the send button instantly sending the SMS out by itself. The fumble-fingered mistake has simply added to his mood. Having just gotten off the phone with his 17 year-old daughter, who was giving him a hard time, he had been hoping to hear a friendly voice. When Sherry didn't immediately respond, he waited half an hour before sending another. This time he very consciously completes the message before hitting "send."

"Sorry to intrude. Hope you and your son are having a great afternoon."

A minute later, he receives a reply: "Hi Tom, so nice to hear from you. We were out for lunch, our little Sunday routine."

"How did it go?"

"Lovely. We got our usual table so Oscar could observe the buses. Now he's out burning calories on the playground. How about you?"

"Nothing special. Just a long phone call with my daughter."

"Nice, what is she up to?"

"She is about to graduate from high school and struggling with what to do afterwards. Lately, we've been having a hard time talking."

"Sorry to hear it. It's such a critical moment in her life. You see her regularly?"

"Not really. Actually, I never did, not even when she was a child. It's a long story."

"No wonder you're having a hard time talking now."

"Any ideas?"

"Talk requires a mutual channel of communication. Maybe you never built one."

"I think it's more me than a channel. We don't speak the same language."

"Don't be silly, Tom. How many clients have you successfully worked with who originally didn't speak 'your' language?"

"Many. Building a strong rapport with difficult clients is one of my strengths."

"That's because you invested time in building a channel."

"Maybe. I never really thought about it in those terms. For me, I've always kept my family and professional lives completely separate."

"How? You mean you are a different person at home than you are at work?"

"No, of course not."

"Then why don't you use your strength for building rapport in both spheres?"

"I don't follow you, Sherry."

"If you are good at engaging with difficult clients, you should be equally good at engaging with a difficult daughter."

"Who said she's difficult?"

"Nobody, Tom. I just used the term to help explain my rationale. Don't get offended so easily."

"I just hate talking about it."

"No problem. We can stop anytime."

"That's not what I meant. It's just hard to talk about it."

"Of course. Because it hurts you."

"No, it doesn't. Why should it hurt me?"

"Come on, Tom."

"All right. Yes, it hurts. Happy now?"

"This is not about me. It's about you. You failed to invest in building this channel of communication between you and your daughter, and now you're paying the price. And don't say you didn't have the time."

"You can really be brutal, Sherry."

"Not brutal, Tom, just honest. You said yourself that you divided your life into the two spheres and invested differently in each. Why shouldn't there be two different outcomes?"

"Good point. I'll let you go now. Thank you, Sherry."

"My pleasure. Take good care."

Ending the texting session, Tom continues to stare at his cell phone lost in thought. At last, he rises and steps out onto his terrace. Clearly soothed by his exchange with Sherry, he begins to whistle as he waters the potted hibiscus.

At the same time, Sherry puts her cell back into her bag and turns to find Oscar just coming back from the monkey bars. Seeing the look on her face, the boy seems puzzled:

"Mommy, why are you smiling?"

Of course there are situations in which the constraints are real. But most often they are a welcome excuse to hide behind and to avoid addressing the root cause of a situation. In fact, we have become very skilled at developing narratives to justify our decisions. And because everybody is using them, it's very tough to unmask the fake constraints they are built on.[3]

By far the most popular narrative to explain today's situation revolves around Mother Nature and the differences supposedly resulting from gender. Of course, only women can give birth, and only women can breastfeed. But does that automatically make them better Caregivers? And of course, if we compare specific physical skills like throwing an object, men outperform women in almost every case.[4] But does that make them automatically more successful Breadwinners particularly in today's economy where approximately 85% of all employees work in services related industries where throwing skills play virtually no part?[5] The answer is obviously no, and a quick reality check confirms the answer: Female Breadwinners and male Caregivers *do* exist in nature, here and today. They are not in the majority, but they do exist, and they do so very successfully and happily. Hence, the pure biological differences between men and women can't explain today's rigid separation into Breadwinners and Caregivers and all the inequalities that come with it.

If it's not purely biological, maybe less tangible gender differences such as one's level of ambition or level of empathy can explain the separation. Are women not ambitious enough to climb the career ladder? Or are men not empathic enough to raise children?

Let's start with ambition. McKinsey & Company, a leading consulting firm, has found that very comparable ambition levels exist between male and female employees.[6] But while the desire to move up the career ladder is equally strong between men and women, the confidence that such upward mobility will actually occur is not. When they asked employees in mid-level and senior management positions if they wished to reach the C-Suite, 81% of men and 79% of women said yes. But when those same employees were asked how confident they are in reaching that goal, women were 20–25% less confident than men. How come? The answer is: women don't trust the system. While they do have confidence in their own qualifications and abilities, they lack confidence that the breadwinner-driven culture of today's workplace will allow them to succeed.

But this has nothing to do with ambition. In fact, there is no gender ambition gap. There is only a convenient fiction designed to preserve the male dominance at work, allowing both—Breadwinners and Caregivers—to elegantly eliminate the option that would make them feel most guilty. This fictional construct allows Breadwinners to justify their limited participation at home because their presumably higher level of ambition makes them predestined to focus on career. And it allows Caregivers to justify their limited participation at work because their presumably lower level of ambition makes them predestined to focus on home and kids.

Let's look if the same logic applies to the claim that men are less empathic than women and hence have a harder time meaningfully engaging with their kids. Why don't we try to see if empathy exists in male behavior somewhere else, for example, at work, where men tend to spend most of their time. We don't have to look far: Mentoring. At its core, mentoring is nothing else but a relationship, a relationship between the mentor and the mentee. Sometimes the relationship is a little closer, sometimes a little looser. Sometimes the relationship turns into friendship, sometimes it stays professional. But for sure it's based on mutual trust and empathy—empathy of the mentor for the mentee's needs for development and encouragement, and empathy of the mentee for the mentor's skills and advice he has to offer. A mentor who doesn't understand his mentee's needs is worthless.

Today, mentoring seems to be the backbone of many corporate careers. In order for this system to work, you need qualified mentors. Hence, it is probably fair to conclude that most prototypical Breadwinners may have carefully guided as many as a dozen mentees while hardly playing any similar role in the lives of their own children.[7] And the reason for this is not a lack of empathy, but a lack of confidence in their abilities to succeed in the caregiver-driven environment at home.

So here we have yet another carefully orchestrated narrative celebrating a gender gap that doesn't exist in nature, only in our heads. In this case, it is designed to preserve the female dominance at home, allowing both—Caregivers and Breadwinners—to adroitly eliminate the option that would make them feel most guilty: It allows Caregivers to justify their limited participation at work, because their presumably higher level of empathy makes them predestined to focus on kids and home. And it allows Breadwinners to justify their limited participation at home, because their presumably lower level of empathy makes them predestined to focus on career.

Unsurprisingly, many scholars have come to the same conclusion, namely that the similarities between the sexes outnumber the differences by far.[8] But in the end, it's up to us to decide what research and which statistics we want to look at, to read and write about, and ultimately believe in. Independent of our decision, reality will continue to speak its own language, and the message is loud and clear: The separation into Breadwinners and Caregivers was invented by humans, not by Mother Nature.

"Hope you're having a great Sunday, Tom! How is life in New York?"

Enjoying a lazy Sunday afternoon at her parents, Sherry is in an upbeat mood as she watches them leave with Oscar for a short stroll around town. Feeling this is the perfect time to check in with Tom after a week of silence, she sends him her text. Sure enough, she doesn't have to wait long for Tom to reply:

"Hello, Sherry. What a pleasant surprise. Life here is good. How about life in Chicago? How is Oscar?"

"Things are good here, too. I'm at my parents, who are enjoying their time with Oscar—and vice versa."

"I take it your parents are in good health?"

"They're very well, thanks. How about yours?"

"Same here. Of course, they are not getting younger."

"But more relaxed, I'll bet. Today my mom really surprised me. She had read an article in the newspaper about gender equality and—."

She is in the middle of completing her thought when Tom interrupts with a text of his own:

"Want me to call you? Might be easier."

Sherry hesitates for a second. But before she can shift gears and start typing her response, her cell rings. It's Tom, who picks up their conversation without missing a beat:

"So she read the article. What did she say?"

"She said that if they would have had a choice, she would have continued working and my dad would have stayed home, not the other way around. I was like: 'Excuse me, Mom, what did you just say?'"

"That's pretty bold for somebody of her generation. Now I know where you get it from!"

"But she was dead serious. She had obviously thought the whole thing through. First, although she had had less of an education than my dad, who used to work in the government sector, she—with her accountant degree—could have easily out-earned him in the long-term by working her way up in the finance department of any large company. Second, she is an extrovert and great with people while he is introvert and shies away from new relationships. So while she would have enjoyed pursuing a career, for him it was always a battle. Third, he was much more patient with kids than she was. You should see him with Oscar."

"Even not knowing them, it sounds like she has a point."

"She absolutely does. I had never thought about it because that's just how I grew up, and she was a wonderful mom, and my dad enabled us to have a beautiful life. But I thought it was quite sweet of her to bring this up."

"Well, confronted with the same decision today, they would have been luckier."

"Maybe."

"Not maybe, for sure. Things have changed quite a bit."

"Things yes, but not our attitudes. Look at yourself."

"Excuse me, Sherry, but what I have done was by choice."

"*Of course* this was by choice, Tom. The only thing I wonder is how all these choices seem to magically happen along the gender line."

"You're very funny, Sherry. Listen, I will be in Chicago in three weeks from now, Wednesday and Thursday. Would you be interested in getting together for a drink?"

"Sure…"

"You pick the place, the drinks are on me. Deal…?"

"Sounds like a deal… I will… Good."

"Yes, very good indeed… Meanwhile, I've asked our

Human Resources Department to provide me with some numbers. I have an idea."

"Idea for what?"

"For what to do with those women's workshops we discussed."

"Oh… I see. Interesting. What about?"

"Too early to share yet. With me you have to learn to be patient."

"All right, whatever!"

"Was very nice talking with you. Good to hear your voice, Sherry. Thanks for reaching out."

"Sure… same here. Bye-bye."

Sherry hasn't felt so excited in a long time. But she is glad to have three weeks of prep time, and so is Tom. He is very satisfied with the way things are evolving, but he needs some time to structure his thoughts. This has all been quite unexpected, and he doesn't like surprises. But this one feels different.

If it's true that gender is not the obstacle, then it should come as no surprise that the majority of corporate initiatives and governmental legislation to foster gender equality have not yielded the results one might expect. Of course, they have their value. Some of them were actually long overdue. But their purpose is to generate equal opportunities for men and women alike. How we leverage them is up to us, as the following example illustrates:

Sweden, world-famous for its progressive approach towards gender equality, was the first country in the world to introduce far-reaching parental leaves. The original law entitled parents to a total of 180 days of leave, paid at 90% of the wage and was to be allocated between both parents as they saw fit. In the first year after the introduction of this law, dads took a bare 0.5% of the total paid parental leave. This was forty years ago.[9]

Since then, the number of days has increased as incentives were built in to encourage more men to take this leave. Consequently today, out of 480 days of leave, 60 days are reserved for dad. That means that mom can take a maximum of 420 days; however, if dad doesn't take his 60 days, they are "lost". The male share of the total paid parental leave has thus increased to 24%.[10]

Now should this make us want to smile or cry? Forty years is quite a long time to adapt, but the burden (or pleasure) of care giving still primarily falls to the woman. So perhaps men really are less interested in raising their kids—not because they are not empathic enough or because of any other manufactured justification, but simply because work interests them more. Or rather, is this actually the result of the unfortunate interplay between two guilty decision makers: A guilty mom, who feels obligated to take most of the leave; and a guilty dad, who gratefully lets her? If this is the case, one thing is for certain: Continuing to point a finger at everybody but ourselves will not solve the problem.

This was also the conclusion that McKinsey arrived at: Eliminating formal constraints is important, but insufficient to achieve real results, because the true constraints are embedded in the culture and legacy of the organizations.[11] Hence one of their suggestions was to focus on training programs—in particular, for the male majority—to help change the culture, rather than introduce more policies or launch more initiatives.

In the end, each of us has to decide what it is that we really want and be honest with one another. It's fine if you want to stay home, but say so. It's fine if you don't really want to spend too much time with the kids, but just say so. Because playing the victim of invented constraints will get us nowhere.

3

When High Performers Underperform

"Oh la-là…! You look spectacular, Sherry!"

It's evening as Tom slips into the seat across from Sherry without taking his eyes off her. Dressed in a stunning black cocktail dress, Sherry smiles, obviously pleased that he noticed… Having chosen a posh, yet low-key bar frequented by a quiet after-work crowd, she is also satisfied with her choice, but Tom couldn't care less. He just keeps staring at her:

"I never saw you dressed like this before… I love your dress. "

"Thank you, Tom, thank you… I usually tone it down for work. Makes life easier."

"Pity."

"Reality. At least for now."

"If you say so. What would you like…?"

"I'll have a glass of Sauvignon Blanc."

Tom orders two glasses of white wine.

"So tell me, Sherry, how did you end up in Chicago?"

"For one, I really like the area. I grew up in Crystal Lake, a small town northwest of the city. Then I went to college at Northwestern and realized how much I enjoyed living in the city. So Chicago became the logical choice. How about you? How did you end up in New York?"

"Work."

"Just work?"

"To be honest, Sherry, I don't care where I live. One place is pretty much as good as another. As long as I'm close to work."

"Really? I couldn't! I need the buzz and the vibes of the city. I enjoy exploring new restaurants, seeing international exhibitions, or doing some serious shopping…"

"When do you have time for all that?"

"It's not a question of having time, Tom, it's a question of making time. Of course, I don't go out that often anymore since Oscar was born. But I still take care of myself. In the end, it's a question of being selective. And believe me, having a child has made me *very* selective."

"You're seriously saying that it's better with a child than without?"

"Absolutely. It's true that with Oscar I'm much more conscious of how I spend my time, so I make the most of it. And having a child always gives you a credible reason to be as selective as you want. Remember how you told me about that period when your wife was in hospital? You had to use your time wisely to get everything done. But it worked."

"True. Necessity is the mother of all childcare."

Sherry laughs, appreciating his sense of humor. She playfully winks at Tom.

"You are so right—at least in my case, but maybe not so much in yours."

"What do you mean?"

"Well, when your wife was in the hospital—out of necessity—you invented a new way of doing your job in order to be able to take care of your kids, right?"

"Right. So what difference does that make?"

"Then—if I remember correctly—when she came home, you went back to your old routine."

"And your point is…?"

"If this new way of working allowed you to do your job as well as spend more time with your kids, I just keep wondering why you would give that up?"

"I knew you were after something… But if I start agreeing with you that this was not the most rational decision I ever made, I might have to start agreeing with everything. And I'm not ready to concede and call it guilt, at least not yet."

"That's fine, Tom. I don't want you to concede anything, I just want you to consider all your options."

She hesitates, then adds: "The truth is I care… and I want you to recognize the gap between what you—I mean, we all—*believe* is happening, and what is *really* happening."

"You can be very sweet, Sherry—"

This time it is Tom who playfully winks at Sherry.

"—when you want to be."

"I take that as a compliment."

"You should… you absolutely should… Speaking of seeing what is really happening reminds me—I got the data from Human Resources and was quite surprised at what I found."

"Tell me."

"Basically, the percentage of men and women who leave the company for a lack of work-life balance is equally high—far too high—for men and women alike, relatively speaking, of course."

"Doesn't surprise me. But it's interesting to hear the facts confirm what I've been thinking."

"It's unacceptable, Sherry." Clearly, Tom's passion about solving the problem is reflected in his tone. "Think about it."

"Of course, it is. But nobody seems to want to face the truth."

"I'm dead serious. We invest so much in developing talent, we simply can't afford to loose them that way… And I don't care how they define the 'personal life' part of the equation—be it for family or sports—or saving endangered turtles…!"

"Calm down, Tom. I'm on your side, remember? I couldn't agree more, but we have to find a way to make everyone understand."

"Yes, *exactly*." Glancing down, he realizes her glass is empty. "Care for another glass of wine?"

"No, thank you. I actually promised Oscar I'd be home before he falls asleep, so I better get going—hope don't mind."

"Of course not…" Smiling, he stands and steps behind her to hold her chair. "Well, actually that's not true. I do mind. But I also respect you for being selective."

"Tom...! Are you making fun of me?"

"Me...? Never." Then breaking into a boyish grin, he adds "Well, maybe sometimes... When I can't help myself. Truth is, it's fun making fun of you, Sherry."

When they step out into the fresh air, Tom takes Sherry's right hand and meets her gaze:

"Thank you for picking the spot and for meeting me. I really enjoyed it."

"Same here."

For an awkward moment, both sense their mutual attraction. Continuing to hold her hand for another short moment, he finally lets her go.

"See you soon."

"I hope so. Good night."

Then with a smile, she turns and moves off. He watches her go before walking off in the opposite direction.

Nobody wants to underperform—yet all of us do from time to time. The question is why? Sometimes it's a pure lack of knowledge, which is the easiest one to fix. Sometimes it's simply a misunderstanding, which is not difficult to fix once you realize the miscommunication. Occasionally, it's a lack of motivation, which can be more problematic to fix but is still manageable. But the most difficult to master is guilt.

Guilt makes us underperform in two distinct ways: Over-delivery and downplay. Over-delivery is when we overcompensate because we feel guilty. Downplay is when we hold ourselves back, even undersell ourselves, because we feel guilty. Each is damaging in its own way and both feed directly into the guilt loop. Let's start with over-delivery.

Over-delivery means spending far too much time on an activity that doesn't add value, an activity that doesn't need to be done. Of course, the relative value of activities differs from person to person. Some women consider wearing make-up a necessity, others a waste of time. Some men consider having a shiny car a necessity, others couldn't care less. All that is fine. The important thing here is—similar to the guilt/satisfaction scale in the previous chapter—that we make conscious well-reasoned decisions. We should be aware of how we spend our time, and why. Do we spend time on an activity because we see a concrete value to it or is it simply because we believe it is expected of us? And this is exactly where guilt comes into play: Guilt makes us do things that we otherwise wouldn't think of doing. In attempting to ease our guilt, we have turned both home and workplace into cultures of over-delivery. Here is how:

If we spend time on something that we *should not* be doing (activity 1), we feel guilty because we could have spent that time on something that we *should* be doing (activity 2). One way of managing the guilt is to spend extra time on activity 2—to compensate for the time we spent on activity 1. And the more guilty we feel, the more we try to compensate.

That's why the quintessential Breadwinner works crazy hours, because just the thought of spending time with the kids makes him already feel guilty. By filling evening and weekend hours with work, the possibility of spending time on kids and household duties doesn't even occur to him. Guilt has been successfully suppressed before it ever comes up. The moderate Breadwinner over-delivers a little less, but makes sure to spend extra time doing work on the evenings when he doesn't have to pick up the kids, to prove that he is still a committed employee.

And that's why the quintessential Caregiver over-engineers child rearing and household management because just the suggestion of spending time away from the kids makes her already feel guilty. By filling every day with child-related activities, the idea of spending time on a career never even comes up. Guilt has been successfully suppressed before it ever arises. The moderate Caretaker over-delivers a little less, but makes sure to stay up late to bake the cupcakes herself, to prove that she is still a good mom.

Again, each of us must decide how we want to spend our time, but it is important to realize that we do have a choice, as the following examples show: Yearly, dozens of studies are done analyzing how we spend our time at work and looking for ways we can spend it more wisely. At the top of every unproductivity list are meetings. The numbers indicating how much wasted time is generated by meetings vary by profession and seniority level, but they are all alarmingly high: Middle managers spend up to 35% of their time in meetings while upper management sometimes allocates as much as 50% of their time.[1] At least half of the time we spend in meetings is considered squandered because many meetings were either unnecessary (think of meetings designated as "to check in" or "to circle back") or poorly prepared and run (think of meetings without a set agenda or meetings that end without a decision). If we do a conservative calculation by applying this to an average 40-hour workweek, we are talking about a weekly waste of six hours, almost a full working day. And if we add the travel time for out-of-town or out-of-country meetings, we talk about even more waste, much more.

Now let's think through a typical example from the home sphere: Cupcakes can be bought (option 1) or made. And they can be made in many different ways from using a simple cupcake mix (option 2) to fully homemade (option 3). Option 1 takes by far the least time; we are talking minutes. Option 2 takes a little longer; we might be talking an hour now, depending on how much practice one has. Option 3 is open ended. We could easily be talking hours to make those all-organic, perfectly iced, and uniquely decorated cupcakes.[2] The difference in time invested by the Caregiver is significant depending on which option she chooses, while the kids will eat them all up within minutes.

Unfortunately, the waste of valuable time is not the main negative impact of over-delivery. Even worse is how over-delivery keeps raising the barrier for entry into the opposite sphere: Long work hours make it even harder for Caregivers to consider taking on a paid job. And equally, over-engineered childrearing makes it even harder for Breadwinners to get seriously involved at home. Let's go back to the cupcakes for a moment: Option 1 can be executed by pretty much anyone. Option 2 can be executed by pretty much anyone who can read the instructions on the package. Option 3 is out of reach for anyone except a dedicated

Caregiver. So the more we feel guilty, the more we over-deliver; and the more we over-deliver, the higher we raise the entry barriers, reinforcing the standard roles of a female Caregiver and male Breadwinner, which makes us feel even guiltier the next time we consider deviating from these norms.

Having said that, if you—female or male—want to make those all-organic, perfectly iced, and uniquely decorated cupcakes, go for it. I will be the first one at the party to ask who made those gorgeous cupcakes and seek you out to compliment you. The two things I'm asking from you is that you don't complain about the time it took you to prepare the cupcakes (because it was your free choice), and that you don't judge the cupcakes that the other parents bring (because that was their free choice).

"Sherry, I have good news."

Tom calls Sherry on his way home from work. It's a crisp, clear evening, the kind—weather permitting—he usually prefers walking to taking a taxi. Sherry is still in the office. She feels a momentary rush at seeing Tom's phone number on her display and almost a little disappointed when she realizes that he is calling about work:

"Tell me."

"I introduced what we've been discussing to the senior partners."

"Really…? That was fast."

"You will learn that once I decide to do something, I move quickly."

"You certainly do. How did it go?"

"Depends on who you ask… it wasn't exactly a smooth ride."

"What? I hope you didn't screw it up. Why didn't you discuss it with me beforehand?"

"Wait, Sherry, wait. I thought you would trust me more by now."

"Please, just tell me what happened."

"All right. I asked for a 15 minute slot and called it 'Retention Optimization.'"

"Sounds sexy." She tries not to sound too sarcastic, but it just slips out. "No wonder nobody wanted to hear you out."

"Sherry, please. I know this topic means a lot to you, but believe me, I'm here to help. And you should know by now that I never do things unplanned. So may I finish?"

"Of course, sorry."

"I purposely made it sound 'unsexy'—to use your language—so nobody would ask me upfront what it was all about. And indeed, nobody did, except for Miss… Retention—I keep forgetting her name—who I managed to elegantly avoid a couple of times in the hallway."

"Susan … Susan something."

"Sounds about right. In any case, here is what I said: First, the real retention problem comes from long and unpredictable work hours. Second, this is not only true for moms, but also for dads, which is worse for a firm like ours because we have many more dads than moms. And therefore, third, we should be investing in those parents who are resilient enough to make it work—who find the proper balance between their commitments at work and home, independent of their gender."

"Wow, I mean, wow. This is quite bold."

"Yes, Madame, it *was* quite bold indeed. And so was the reaction. Valerie stood up and walked straight out of the room without saying a word. That was not very helpful. And I told her so afterwards when I went to see her in her office."

"She does overreact sometimes. But in this case, I can understand it. She probably expected you to talk it over with her first."

"But that's exactly what I did *not* want to do. If I had, it would have automatically been dismissed by the men in the room as yet another women's initiative."

"True."

"So if we want real change, we have to do things differently. Everything we do, including how we communicate."

"I guess I agree. I'm just not sure *how* differently we will have to do things."

"Very differently, Sherry, very differently. Otherwise we run the risk of just doing more of the same."

"Okay, okay. So at this point there must have been only guys left, right?"

"No, we also have Pat."

"True, I keep forgetting about her. She keeps such a low profile."

"And she doesn't have kids, so she couldn't care less. But she actually made a very thoughtful comment at the end. She is a fine person."

"Who else commented?"

"Wait, my impatient lady, let me first finish the story. Here is what I said next: I'm seriously pissed. I keep losing one good guy after another—guys I carefully hired and trained, and who performed up to my standards. And the reason why I lose them is because some of you in this room scope and manage your projects in a way that requires them to work crazy hours. Then I paused and looked at each of them before I said: So I keep hearing about all those women's initiatives and how they train women to speak up and encourage them to organize work around their kids. And I actually think the same approach would be equally powerful for guys as well."

"I see… Not exactly what I expected, but it works… works actually quite nicely."

"For a while the room was quiet. Finally, I closed by saying: I would like us to think about it and leverage what we can learn from the women's initiatives, then come up with a fresh solution."

"Very elegant, Tom… So who broke the ice?"

"Arjun. He knew exactly who I was referring to when I talked about the crazy work hours. He hates them as much as I do. And then Pat stepped in and said that she would welcome the opportunity to finally take on the real problems—such as work-life balance—from a general perspective, rather than a gender perspective."

"That's exactly our point!"

"Yes it is, my dear… Now it's your baby. In order to make sure all these guys don't backslide, we'll need data to prove that what we are claiming is actually true. It will be tricky to lure them out of their comfort zone, but I think I paved the way."

"All right, then let me take over."

"I'm really excited, Sherry. If we can make this work, it will solve so many problems and annoyances – and save money…" Clearly on a roll, Tom decides to take a chance and raise their relationship to the next level. "Listen, we obviously make a good team. I couldn't have done this without you. I'd like to see you again."

Caught off guard, she hesitates.

Sensing this, Tom quickly adds: "This time I want dinner. I'll ask my assistant to send over some possible dates. You pick one and let me know. Gotta jump. I'm just walking up to my front door. You take care."

"You too. Let's stay in touch."

Downplay is the second form of guilt-driven underperformance, the other side of the coin so to speak. Here is what we've already learned: If we spend time on something that we *should not* be doing (activity 1), we feel guilty because we could have better spent that time on something that we *should* be doing (activity 2). One way of managing the guilt is to spend extra time on activity 2—to compensate for the time spent on activity 1. The other way to manage guilt is to hold ourselves back and downplay the importance of our contribution to activity 1 thereby making our contribution to activity 2 stand out. And the more guilty we feel, the more we hold ourselves back.

This time, let's start with the Caregivers to see how this

plays out in reality. It's a well-established fact that Caregivers and Caregivers-to-be still earn less than Breadwinners and Breadwinners-to-be for doing the same job. But why? The answer lies in part with the Caregivers themselves: they simply don't ask for more. A study among MBA graduates found that only 7% of potential future Caregivers attempted to negotiate their first salary after graduation compared to 57% of potential future Breadwinners. Unsurprisingly, this led to an 8% difference between their starting salaries.[3]

Why don't Caregivers ask? Of course nobody will give them a higher salary if they don't ask. That's the rule of the game, independent of gender. Maybe they are just too shy to ask. Or maybe they are worried they will be perceived as pushy. Hard to believe, because Caregivers turn into great negotiators and couldn't care less about being pushy when it has to do with their kids. So either Caregivers aren't concerned about their salary or it's guilt that makes them hold back and downplay their value and contribution in the workplace.

Now let's turn to the Breadwinners: Here we don't have a pay gap, but a flexibility gap. You have never heard of the flexibility gap? No wonder, because nobody ever writes or talks about it. But in essence it's the mirror image of the pay gap: It's a well-known fact that Breadwinners still make less use of flexibility offered at work than Caregivers do, despite the fact that many of them have full-time working spouses and hence the same theoretical share of responsibility for kids and chores. Similar to the Caregivers, the answer lies, in part, with the Breadwinners themselves: they simply don't ask for more. And flexibility could mean many things, from part-time work to flexible work arrangements to other new ways of gaining additional flexibility and predictability over their work hours. But the only times Breadwinners typically ask for flexibility is for their wedding, their honeymoon, and maybe for a few days after the baby is born.[4]

Why don't Breadwinners ask? Of course, nobody will give them more flexibility if they don't ask. Again, that's the rule of the game, independent of gender. Maybe they are just too shy to ask. Or maybe they are worried about being perceived as pushy. This is equally hard to believe, because Breadwinners turn into great negotiators and couldn't care less about being seen as pushy when it's about their salary or a promotion. So either Breadwinners don't care about their kids or it's guilt that makes them hold back and downplay the value of their contribution at home.

Unfortunately, downplaying our value has much bigger implications than just the immediate loss of money or flexibility. Every woman who earns less than her spouse will be inclined to be the primary Caretaker. And every man who has less flexibility than his spouse will be inclined to be the primary Breadwinner. So the more we feel guilty, the more we downplay our value; and the more we downplay our value, the bigger the gap we create between the spouses with respect to salary and flexibility, reinforcing the standard roles of a female Caregiver and male Breadwinner, which makes us feel even guiltier the next time we deviate from them.

4

The Grand Delusion We All Fall For

"Happy Sunday, Sherry! What are you up to?"

Tom is home, watching the Giants take on the Patriots on TV. But his thoughts keep going back to Sherry in that dress.

Sherry, however, has taken her son Oscar to a kid's birthday party in Lincoln Park where he's had a run-in with a playmate. Thus when Tom's SMS arrives, she first must tend to Oscar's needs before she can reply:

"I'm at one of those all-pink birthday parties."

"Sounds fun!"

"Well, it's cute to see the kids having fun… and it's good to catch up with some of the parents… but it's just a little too much for my taste."

"Like what? I've never participated in such a party."

"Not even the ones for your own children?"

"Not that I can remember. They usually were in the afternoon during the week and I had to work."

"The parties differ quite a bit. We've had everything—from jump castles to magicians to arts and crafts parties, like the one today."

"So what is pink then?"

"The cake, the decorations... You have no idea how far some parents go... Even the goodie bags are color-coded: Pink for the girls, blue for the boys."

"I see. I guess they want to prepare them for the real world!"

"This is not a funny joke, Tom! This whole pink- and blue-mania is really disturbing. Recently Oscar asked me if the pink ice cream truck around the corner is for girls only! Can you imagine?"

"No."

"I really wonder what message we are sending our kids..."

"My guess is that parents don't realize what they are doing."

"That's even more disturbing. Like a disease that you don't realize you have."

"Does Oscar like pink?"

"Yes, he does! When the online shop mistakenly delivered a pink and a blue water bottle instead of the two blue ones I ordered, he only wanted to drink from the pink one."

"Sounds to me like you are infected with the same disease, Sherry."

"I'm afraid I am. I was worried about the other kids' reaction when he'd show up with a pink water bottle. But he couldn't care less..."

"Good, good for him... I'd say Oscar's got style. This

reminds me of our last company summer outing when I decided to wear my pink pants. You wouldn't believe the looks I got! Let Oscar chose the colors he fancies as long as he can handle the reactions."

"That's what I'm trying to do now."

"You should… So then the presents must be all pink, too!"

"The wrapping paper, yes, the contents I'm not so sure. They haven't opened them."

"I see."

"You really have no clue about birthday parties, Tom!"

"I told you… Are there any dads at the party?"

"Of course there are, quite a few actually."

"Interesting."

"Why is this interesting?"

"Because I'd never go."

"But it's a Sunday afternoon."

"True. Still. In my experience, birthday parties are a room full of screaming kids and chattering moms—not a place for me. That was their mother's domain."

"And when you had them for a Sunday afternoon, what did you do with your kids?"

"Actually, they prefer spending Sunday afternoons with their friends rather than with their dad."

"I meant when they were at Oscar's age."

"That depends. I took them to the playground, the zoo, maybe a movie…"

"Okay. So what's the difference between the playground and a birthday party?"

"Uh-oh, my dear Sherry. I get the feeling there's another bold statement coming up."

"You better watch out, Tom!"

"Okay. We'll just leave it at that for now. The Giants are in the Red Zone. I need to get back to my game."

"Sure. And I'll go and chat… with some of the dads."

"Don't make me jealous, please!"

"Don't make me laugh, please!"

"Have you booked the restaurant yet?"

"I will tonight."

"All right, take good care. Nice texting with you, as always."

"Very nice indeed."

Sherry puts her cell away, still smiling over Tom's comment, and goes back to mingling with some of the parents.

Tom turns the volume back up on the television and tries to concentrate on the game. He still can't quite believe how Sherry seems to have just walked into his life, unannounced. Reminding himself this is only the beginning, he is smart enough to keep things in perspective. But even so, it feels right.

Once we realize how guilt manipulates us, we begin to wonder how we ever allowed it to play such a large part in our lives. Because one thing is certain: No one would voluntarily sign up to be trapped in this kind of "guilt-loop," but no one seems to be immune to it. So how did we get here in the first place?

The answer is the "Grand Delusion" that we are all seduced by: The delusion that we live in a free society with all options open. The delusion suggests that we can achieve whatever we desire, if we just work hard enough. Naturally, each of us has a different starting point, and some of us have to work a little harder than others to achieve our goals, but the world is accessible to everyone. Think of it as one big pipeline that we all enter the day we are born, a big wide pipeline. With each passing year the pipeline is divided into smaller passageways, reflecting the diverging skills and interests of each of us as we develop: Some are into sports, some into music. Some are better with numbers, some with languages. Some care more about aesthetic solutions, some about pragmatic ones. Some are capable of making bold decisions early on, some need to keep exploring a while longer before deciding. Some prefer to work with many people, some on their own. Some want to have kids, some do not. But the most significant misconception about this pipeline is that all options are open to everyone, guilt-free.

The reality looks completely different. In reality there are *two* pipelines. One is pink and one is blue. The pink one is designed to develop future Caregivers, the blue one to develop future Breadwinners. The day we are born, girls are automatically fed into the pink pipeline and boys into the blue one. Of course, everyone is welcome to switch from one pipeline to the other—but not without feeling guilty. Unfortunately, there is no third pipeline, a "neutral pipeline" so to speak. The options are only one or the other—pink or blue. And as a result, we all find ourselves caught up in the guilt-loop.

"Lara Croft…?"
Tom is almost shouting into his cell phone, he still can't believe it. Sherry holds the phone away from her ear, wondering why he is shouting:
"Hello, Tom…? Is this you?"
"Yes, it's me, Sherry. Can you please explain this to me?"
"What are you talking about, Tom?"
"I'm talking about the Lara Croft action figure!"
"Wow, that was fast. It barely took four weeks!"
"So you are the one behind this?"
"Of course. How did you hear about it?"
"The guys on other teams are taking selfies with this doll and sending it to their colleagues. That's how it ended up in my team."
Unable to keep a straight face, Sherry starts to laugh.
"Brilliant. I couldn't have asked for more."
"Sherry, can you please tell me what is going on?"
"With pleasure. I wanted to prove that we are working on a real, not an imagined problem. So I started looking for a way to get the guys in the office to speak for themselves. At first, I was thinking that we could penalize the last guy to leave for the night. But I decided that a more positive approach might work better, a sort of 'early bird' trophy for the guy who finishes his work and goes home first."
"Smart idea…"
"Let me finish. So during a recent lunch with my team I

started a casual discussion around work hours and suggested we make it a little competition. They picked right up on it. And once we had defined the rules, I made them pick out a trophy to go to the winner. Of course, I guided the discussion a little bit by rejecting any boring proposals. Whatever they decided on, I wanted it to be bold."

"A Lara Croft, Tomb Raider, action figure…? I'd say you definitely achieved your goal. So what are the rules?"

"Very simple. Every evening we track who goes home first. The one who goes home first most often each week wins the trophy. This allows for someone who decides to work until midnight one evening to still be in the running to win the trophy."

"But how on earth did they come up with Lara Croft?"

"It's not a bad choice, Tom. Lara is the first real heroine in the world of video games. She stands for intelligence and independent decisions. She is sexy, which can't hurt given our target group. But best of all, it is a doll!"

"With boobs that are right in your face."

Sherry laughs again.

"What did you expect, Tom? She's a woman. They're part of the package."

"Oh, don't get me wrong. I like them… especially on a woman… I mean, generally speaking, of course. Do we really need to talk about this?"

"Why not? I really want to understand what your problem is with her boobs?"

"It's not just her boobs… it's the way she is dressed. Come on Sherry, you know what I'm talking about."

"Of course I do. But who told me recently that it is a pity that I don't dress—let's say—in a more feminine way for work? That's exactly what Lara does… of course applying the dress code of her specific industry."

"I see your point… but just let me say it's a delicate balance."

"Yes, it is, Tom. But all I care about at the moment is that the Lara Croft trophy is perceived positively and not ridiculed. That was the main goal, and I think I can say I achieved it. But what I found really amazing is how the work dynamics within the team have changed since we introduced the trophy."

"Doesn't surprise me. That's what Arjun and I try to teach our clients, day in, day out… to be more efficient. There's just so much wasted time and energy… but to fix it, you first need to see the waste."

"It isn't because it's hard to see, Tom; it's because we don't want to see it. And it's easier to keep repeating our mistakes than it is to change. "

"All right, let's give it some time and see where this whole Lara Croft thing takes us—if anywhere…"

"I'll let you go, grumpy man!"

"Who are you calling grumpy?"

Pleased that he took her teasing the right way, she laughs once more.

"And thank you also for sending over the restaurant address. I'm looking forward to seeing you again… soon."

"Same here."

Sherry's cheeks are glowing when she hangs up. She hasn't felt so enthusiastic in a long time.

Tom, however, has mixed emotions. No question, Sherry's way of creating awareness is brilliant, but very different from how he might have done it, himself. Even so, it's hard not to be impressed.

One of the defining features of being in a pipeline is that one thing feeds into the next, that the current experience builds on the previous one. Hence, in order for each of us to maximize our opportunities, it is crucial to keep as many options open for as long as possible. Let me explain: If we create broad exposure, in particular at the beginning of the pipeline, we keep all our options open. However, if we limit the exposure, for whatever reasons, we preclude certain options right from the get-go. And unfortunately, that's exactly what is happening.

Let's take a closer look at the blue pipeline and try to understand how we inadvertently channel boys into *not* becoming future Caregivers. One of the first experiences newborns have, after meeting mom and dad, is their exposure to toys. But despite all the talk about gender equality and "having it all", the market for toys is still hugely segregated into pink and blue, in fact the level of gender segregation has never been higher.[1] And unless you disagree with the dynamics of supply and demand, this reflects the toys we parents want to buy for our kids. Or is it rather what our kids demand?

It's hard to recognize and even harder to acknowledge,

the true driver behind our buying decisions. And it's much easier to hide behind our kids' demands and put the burden on them. But let's face it, even if your child does have strong preferences, which most of them do and should have, we still have the option to offer them a broader range of choices. Now don't get me wrong, of course it doesn't make sense to continue buying dolls for a boy who shows a decided preference for cars.[2] But why don't we buy him a doll and create the option, allowing the boy himself to decide when and how he wants to play with the doll. Maybe not daily, maybe not even weekly, maybe only once a month. And maybe he doesn't cuddle and feed it, but rather prefers giving it a ride in one of his cars. But that's okay, as long as he doesn't perceive playing with a doll as something negative or strange, or even forbidden, but simply as something natural. This will allow those boys who want to play with a doll to do so without any social stigma attached. At the same time, those boys who prefer other toys will at least not feel uncomfortable when dolls are included in play.

Many of us, however, reject or resist offering such an option, even when the boy asks for it. A popular way to circumvent a boy's wish for a dollhouse, for example, is to buy him a toy barn. It offers the same functionality, but doesn't necessarily require dolls. Of course, when role-playing is involved, the boy may be forced to turn dad into the cow and mom into the horse (or the other way around)—a small sacrifice for parents who are adamant that their son doesn't play with dolls. Alternatively, smart toy manufacturers have come up with other boy-friendly options such as the "monster mansion", turning mom and dad into monsters—but again, who cares, as long as the boy doesn't play with dolls. Then there are the ones among us who do create the option but attach a message to it to make sure the boy is aware that dolls aren't really for boys: "Sweetie, here is the doll stroller you asked for. But we bought it in blue, so your friends don't think you look like a girl." And finally, there are those among us who seriously want to create the option but struggle to do so because they can't find a non-pink dollhouse.

So let me ask you, why are we *so* afraid for boys to play with dolls? Maybe dolls make them soft? Even turn them into little wimps? Or maybe dolls make them caring, causing them to focus on people rather than cars? Maybe they could start caring too much? Fall in love with the doll? Even have second thoughts about the doll? Of course, not. I'm just putting the question out there to show the absurdity of our behavior. Even the famous male monkeys from the research experiment play with dolls from time to time, although they prefer trucks.[3] So it's the most natural thing to do. But the truth is, we don't want boys to become Caregivers.

A few years later, our behavioral pattern repeats itself: Babysitting is a quite smart and well-paid job for teenagers. It's smart, in particular compared to jobs such as washing cars or mowing lawns because it is usually done in the evening hours and often leaves time for private activities once the baby is sleeping. Unsurprisingly, teenage boys are becoming interested in the job, but they frequently are having a hard time being hired. The only time boys are welcome to look after the baby is when it's their own sibling.[4]

So let me ask you again, why are we *so* afraid of having boys babysit? Teenage girls can be little monsters, too. And I would expect any parent to do thorough due diligence (for example, calling the school for feedback) on whomever they trust to care for their baby, independent of gender. But again the truth is, we don't want boys to become Caregivers.

After carefully keeping the boys away from dolls, and after routinely excluding teenage boys from babysitting, are we really surprised when young men don't want to get involved with their own kids once they become fathers? After all, it's what we've been teaching them, and what many of us were taught when we were young. I would call it: Mission accomplished.

"Thank you for a wonderful evening, Sherry. As always, you've been charming—and if I may say again—you look stunning this evening."

Tom motions to the waiter for the check. When it arrives, it is put in front of him. She smiles and lets him take care of it:

"You will learn that with respect to paying the bill, I'm ultra traditional."

"How come?"

"No clue, it just feels right for the man to pay. You might not believe it, but at college I would actually give my boyfriend the money upfront so that he could pay with my money."

"I'd say that's rather special…" Having paid with a credit card, Tom smiles as he rises and holds her chair. "In fact, you're a rather special woman… Ready?"

"Yes, ready for some fresh air. Thank you, Tom."

"You're welcome, my dear."

Once they are out on the street, Tom asks Sherry:

"Do you realize, Sherry, that you don't seem to mind anymore when I call you 'my dear'?"

"You noticed."

"I told you, I pay attention to details."

"And I wonder how many other women you call 'my dear.'"

Responding to Sherry's comment, Tom sees it as the perfect excuse to put his arm around her, teasing her as they begin to walk:

"Don't tell me you're jealous, Sherry?"

"I don't know if I'd call it jealous, but what I know for sure is that you flirt a lot."

"That's not true."

"Yes, it is. You've been doing it all evening."

"Define flirting."

"It's just the way you interact with other women. The way you talk to them, the way you smile at them."

"Really…? Funny woman! You remind me of a conversation I recently had with my youngest, the little boy. We were out for lunch. On our way home he sad: 'Daddy, why are you always being so nice to women?' And I said: 'Because that's the way a gentleman treats a lady. Let me ask you: Would you prefer a dad who was always rude to women?'"

"And what did he say?"

"'Absolutely not.' So I added: 'Then you better make sure you learn from your dad.'"

"Okay, Tom, maybe you're right. I just don't know you well enough yet."

"Fair enough. Take all the time you need."

He gives her shoulder a friendly squeeze:

"You know you really are a beautiful person, Sherry. Not just your looks, everything. Your personality, your values, your imagination… your courage… I'm really impressed."

Sherry cuddles a little closer. It feels good. They stroll for a while in silence. Then Tom says with a twinkle in his eye:

"You must have been really something as student, Sherry—"

"How did you come up with *that*?"

"I was just imagining you going out with that cheap boyfriend."

"He was not cheap. We were just both on a student budget, so we shared the cost of going out."

Teasingly she elbows him in the ribs. Enjoying her playfulness, he continues to keep his arm around her.

"So how do you explain your *'ultra* traditional' need—as you put it—for men to pay when they take you out? I would be curious to know what else you expect them to pay for?"

"No, no, no. Just for dinner… and only when we go out."

"Got it… How about women? If you go out with a girlfriend, you also expect her to pay for you?"

"Tom, please. Of course not."

"Just checking."

"And just for the record, I don't expect all men to pay for me… only the ones I'm romantically involved with."

The moment Sherry finishes her sentence, she realizes what she's just said, but it's too late. Tom stops walking and turns her towards him, holding her shoulders with both hands. For a long moment, he considers her words, then asks:

"So, just for the record, are you suggesting we're romantically involved?"

Without waiting for an answer, he softly kisses her on the forehead before turning around and hailing a taxi. Then he turns back to her:

"Before we go any further, Sherry, you better carefully consider where this might lead. I'm not an easy man."

"That much I've already figured out."

Tom grins as he opens the taxi door allowing Sherry to slip into the backseat. Instinctively, she waves him goodbye through the closed window. But her brain is already working. How could she be so wrong? Or maybe she wasn't?

At the same time, Tom decides to walk back to his hotel. He is proud of himself to have held back. It seems just too good to be true. He needs one more data point.

Let's switch to the pink pipeline, and begin with a quick look at the output of the pipeline because the dynamics are slightly different than in the blue one. Obviously, in today's world, many more girls become full-time Breadwinners than boys become full-time Caregivers. Hence, the pink pipeline is less about carefully channeling girls *not* to become future breadwinners, but it's about channeling them not to become the *main* breadwinner—otherwise, who would do the caregiving?

Channeling girls into in the pink pipeline happens in a more subtle way. It's okay for girls to play with toys traditionally considered to be exclusively for boys. Today, you find Legos or Playmobil toys in almost any girl's bedroom (the pink version, of course). It's okay for girls to play sports originally considered to be only for boys. The female version of these sports doesn't receive the same attention in media as the boy's version, but the options to practice and play most sports exist and are exercised. So the channeling is not so much about excluding options for girls; rather it is about not encouraging girls to pursue certain options. It is almost like allowing these options to slip away unnoticed.

With that in mind, let's go back to the beginning of the pink pipeline, to the early years at school. When girls start primary school, they are as strong in math as boys are. But by the time they finish high school, the boys have surpassed them. What happens in-between? And why does this phenomenon only take place in some countries, but not in all? According to the 2012 PISA study, out of 65 countries, boys outperform girls in math in 37 countries, girls outperform boys in 5 countries, and in the other 23 countries we don't observe a math gender gap. How come?[5]

The math myth—that boys are naturally better at math than girls—has triggered much research, and the results are all the same: There is no significant difference between boys and girls with respect to talent, but there is a difference with respect to performance. Let me explain: Believing that such a difference exists can actually produce that difference in reality. Beliefs are created and nurtured in many ways. That's where the channeling comes into play.[6]

Of course it's intriguing to hide behind our child's apparent preferences in order to avoid confronting the reality. But even if our child does demonstrate strong preferences, which most of them do and should, we have the opportunity, if not the obligation, to encourage them to explore subjects that they might not be drawn to or may even be afraid of. Now don't get me wrong. Of course, it doesn't make sense to continue forcing a girl (or a boy, for that matter) to invest extra time and energy in math if it's simply not her (or his) strength. In that case, it might be more productive to invest that time and energy in a subject where the girl is capable of excelling. However, at the same time, by creating an environment that conveys an excitement for math and underlines its importance in today's world we allow the girl to decide for herself how much she wants to invest. Maybe she does prefer literature or languages or fashion, but that doesn't mean that she has to be poor in math. And maybe she doesn't enjoy solving one math puzzle after the other, but she leverages math to optimize her next shopping trip to the fashion mall: "How many more T-shirts can I buy if I buy discounted ones? And how much time do I need to cover all the stores so I can tell dad when to pick us up?" But that's okay, as long as she doesn't perceive math as an annoyance, as something that others are good at, but she is not. By presenting math in a positive light, we allow those girls who want to focus on math to do so, and those who prefer other subjects to at least feel at ease with it.

Many of us, however, don't create that encouraging environment, not even when the girl shows a real aptitude for math. Often it is well meant but thoughtless adult conversations overheard by the girl that can send the wrong message. For example: Mom A: "Oh, she is so great at handling the little ones at Girl Scouts." Mom B: "You must be so proud of her. Girls just tend to be better with people than with numbers, I see it with my own kids." Mom B has no idea if Girl A is good at math or not, she just assumes that she is not. So what is the message to Girl A? If she is good at math, the message is that she is not normal. And if she is not good at math, the message is that it is okay because she is not expected to be. In either case, the adult conversation pushes the girl away from math, not towards it.

Then there are those among us who do create a math-encouraging environment, but are not consistent in the way they execute it. For example, if the girl comes home with a mediocre math test result, the reaction is more tolerant: "Don't worry, next time you'll do better." If the boy comes home with the same mediocre math test result, the reaction is less tolerant: "This is not acceptable, let's see how you can improve." And finally there are the ones among us who do their best to create and execute a math-encouraging environment, but who have a hard time explaining to the girl why most language teachers happen to be female, and most math and science teacher happen to be male.[7]

So let me ask you, why are we *so* ignorant when it comes to encouraging girls to do well in math? Maybe we feel that math makes them too analytical? Perhaps we feel that it even turns them into little cold-blooded calculators rather than caring moms? Or maybe math makes them too smart? So smart that they might intimidate and out-earn the boys? Could it be that we don't want that? Of course, not. I'm just putting the question out there to show the absurdity of our behavior. Unfortunately, we can't leverage the monkey research this time, as monkeys can't do math. But the truth is, because we don't foresee girls becoming the main Breadwinners, their being good in math is simply seen as irrelevant.

A few years down the road our behavioral pattern repeats itself: In rich countries, more than 60% of the degrees in humanities, and more than 70% of the degrees in health and education are awarded to women, while the majority of degrees in science, technology, engineering and math (STEM) go to men. The implications for the job market and the relative salaries are well known. The implications for the role allocation in the household once the first child is born are clear as well.[8]

So let me ask you again, why are we *so* reluctant for girls to pursue a degree that will earn them more money and greater independence or at least get them a decent job? The answer once more is that we don't anticipate girls becoming the main Breadwinners, and hence their job outlook and salary projections are irrelevant.

After allowing girls to avoid a serious study of math in school, and after passively accepting their choice of seeking a non-STEM degree, are we really surprised when young women don't want to pursue a career outside the home once they become a mother? After all, it's what we've been teaching them, and what many of us were taught when we were young. I would again call it: Mission accomplished. That's why we have two pipelines and not one, and that's why we keep celebrating the gender differences, one baby shower at a time.

PART 2

What Happens When Tom
and Sherry Join Forces:
The rise of a new majority

5

What We Have in Common with Smokers

"Where is my Happy Sunday note, Sherry?"

Tom isn't sure if he should be worried or annoyed. But if the little routine that he and Sherry have developed around Sunday notes still holds true, it should be her turn today. And he finds himself feeling a bit put off that she is making him wait.

"Hello, Mr. Impatient. It's only 2 p.m.!"

"Hello, Ms. Silent! I usually get my note in the morning!"

"I'm not more silent than usual."

"Yes, you are."

"I'm just having a slow Sunday. What's the problem?"

"Nothing. I was just trying to make sense of the unusual silence."

"Good luck with that!"

"Come on, Sherry, don't be nasty."

"Who is the nasty one?"

"I don't appreciate your tone. What did I do? I feel I deserve to know after the beautiful evening we spent together."

"You didn't do anything."

"So?"

"So what?"

"Sherry, please, I'm too old for such games. Tell me what's the problem."

"There is no problem, Tom. Just that on Thursday night—I felt rejected."

"Wow, I mean Wow! How do you come up with *that*?"

"You know exactly what I'm talking about."

"No, I do not. Seriously, please tell me. I thought we had a wonderful evening. In particular, our walk, the fresh air, everything felt so… intimate. The exact opposite of rejection!"

Hitting "send" Tom waits for Sherry to reply. After a couple of minutes, he texts her again.

"Hello? Sherry?"

"I'm here. I just don't know what to say."

Tom decides to call her. Seeing his number displayed on her cell, she lets it ring several times before hitting "accept." She then waits for him to speak first.

"Sherry…?"

"Tom."

Hearing the subdued tone of her voice, he tries again.

"Want to tell me what's the matter?"

"It's just the other night—the way you said good-bye."

"What did I say wrong?"

"You were just so cold, so abrupt… after such a cozy evening… I even hate talking about it, Tom."

"You want to hang up?"

"No… no, I… It just made me wonder how serious you are."

"Excuse me?"

Attempting to control her emotions, Sherry says nothing, which only provokes Tom more.

"Now I'm getting really upset. Are you actually questioning my seriousness? Open your eyes and look at the facts, Sherry! It's the second time I'm flying into your town just for *you*! Do you think I have anything else to do in Chicago?"

"All right, Tom."

"No, it's not all right, Sherry… not at all. I really have no clue what you are talking about. Are there any rules out there that indicate how serious somebody is depending on how he or she says goodbye?"

"Of course not."

"So?"

"Well… It's not about 'goodbye.' It's about the question of the first kiss, which I personally think should be something beautiful… romantic…"

"Question about the first kiss…? What question?"

"You really don't know…?"

"Really."

"Typically, assuming a couple is attracted to one another,

after the first or second date there is the question of the first kiss—picking the right moment."

"I see… So you're suggesting that if this first kiss doesn't happen after the first or second date, then the… encounter is perceived as not serious. Correct?"

When Sherry doesn't reply, Tom takes it for a "yes."

"Not perceived serious by whom? By you, Sherry? By your curious friends? By your impatient mom? Or maybe by the American public in general?"

Stung by his sarcastic tone, Sherry still doesn't answer. Tom presses ahead.

"Do you realize how absurd what you are saying sounds…? Let me tell you my version."

"Please do."

"Last Thursday, I wasn't quite sure what to make of the last thing you said to me just as you were leaving. Do you remember? You implied that by allowing me to pick up the check, we were becoming—in your words—'romantically involved.'"

"Yes I remember."

"So… was it just a sweet slip of the tongue, or were you trying to convey a message? I honestly couldn't tell. So I decided to play it safe."

"It was just a slip, Tom… I don't know if it was sweet or not, but for sure it was a slip."

Neither speaks as the awkwardness of the moment stretches between them. At last, Sherry breaks the impasse.

"I'm so sorry, Tom… I guess I misread it. I must have been

feeling too comfortable with you… I don't know what to say… I'm truly sorry."

"No worries, Sherry. I just didn't want to mess up what we have been carefully building together by moving too fast… You matter to me."

"And you matter to me, too… I guess that's how I began worrying in the first place."

"Well, then let *me* apologize for sending the wrong signal. That was absolutely not my intention."

Wishing he were able to say this to her face instead of over the phone, Tom lowers his voice and tries again.

"My sweet Sherry, I'm glad we talked. I had absolutely no clue what was going on in your mind."

"I'm glad we talked, too. Thank you."

"Take care of yourself," Tom adds. "I'll call you."

"That would be wonderful. Have a nice Sunday."

As both hang up, Tom shakes his head. With so much to mull over, he decides to take a walk and clear his head.

Sherry calls to Oscar and suggests they go to the zoo.

Albert Einstein once said that you cannot solve a problem with the same mind-set that created it. In other words, you have to reframe the problem in order to solve it. We are halfway there. The first step was to expose the root cause of the problem, to realize that it is guilt not gender that is keeping us from having it all. The next step is to understand how we can remove that guilt, how we can overcome it?

As we have learned, guilt is a question of perception. We feel guilty every time we perceive ourselves in the minority going against a moral standard defined and supported by the majority. However, once a standard looses the support of the majority, we no longer feel guilty for being at odds with it. So how does a standard loose the support of the majority? Quite simply by becoming less attractive than a new, emerging standard.

Remember the example we touched upon in Chapter One, smoking? That's exactly what happened there. For a long time, smoking was in vogue. It was perceived as a lifestyle choice, and the majority of people perceived it as a cool choice, independent of whether or not they were smokers. Virtually every movie portrayed its hero or heroine smoking, from Humphrey Bogart to James Dean and from Rita Hayworth to Audrey Hepburn. And who can remember a mystery novel without a chain-smoking detective? Smokers dominated most private and public spaces. The concept of non-smoking was basically non-existent.

Today, however, smoking is considered an evil—a danger to yourself as well as to the people around you. The formerly oh-so-cool smokers are now treated like lepers, struggling to find a spot where they are still allowed to satisfy their need for nicotine. The stigma against smoking has become so great that companies like the giant drugstore chain CVS has decided to stop selling tobacco products in order to improve their public image despite a sizeable revenue loss. Even the tobacco industry itself is now restricting the use of its products as the recent decision to phase out smoking in their offices by R.J. Reynolds, manufacturer of the popular Camel cigarettes, demonstrates.[1] So what convinced people to switch sides and create the critical mass necessary to establish this new standard?

Oddly enough, smokers were actually never in the numerical majority. At its peak, only about 45% of the population smoked.[2] Of course, one single smoker is sufficient to pollute a room with the pungent odor of burning tobacco. But shouldn't that have undermined rather than elevated the status enjoyed by smokers? Then what was it that enabled them to set the standard? It was this perception of coolness, even an air of glamour, that came with smoking that made it seem attractive to smokers and non-smokers alike.[3]

So if both, smokers and non-smokers, constituted the majority, then who was the minority? It was those non-smokers who *did* mind the smoke. But they first had to recognize that their need for change was greater than passive acceptance. Until that point, non-smoking had been considered more a condition than a choice. Secondhand smoke wasn't even part of the vocabulary.[4] Only once they formulated their need for a smoke-free environment, arguing that secondhand smoke was indeed unhealthy, did non-smoking become a conscious choice. And once it became a conscious choice, people could begin to take sides.[5]

Having established the need, it should have been an easy conversion. The number of non-smokers had steadily increased since the first warnings about the health risks of smoking issued in 1964 by America's Surgeon General. By 1980, non-smokers made up 67% of the population versus 33% who continued to smoke. But there were two complicating factors: First, finding a solution that would satisfy both parties was almost impossible given the existence of secondhand smoke. A space is either 100% smoke-free or it's not. Just having *less* smoke doesn't resolve the problem. This didn't leave smokers much choice and created some serious resistance, not only from smokers, but also from non-smokers, many of whom still saw a certain coolness to smoking or felt uncomfortable imposing their own personal choice on others, or both. Second, there was and still is a specialized industry that makes money producing and selling cigarettes, and they didn't want to loose the business. As a result, smokers were supported by a "silent" partner with strong interests and deep pockets.

But ultimately these forces could only slow down, not prevent the majority from implementing the new standard. By the time the first comprehensive indoor smoking ban was in place in America, the number of smokers had already decreased by 40% from its peek. So it was not the law that fostered non-smoking, rather it was the shifting perception of smoking that was turning non-smoking into the more attractive choice. And the more non-smokers started to claim their right to a smoke-free environment, the less attractive smoking became (at least in public). Implementing the law was just the final step in enforcing the new standard as the legislative landscape began to catch up with the new majority. Today 80% of the states have laws in place that restrict smoking in private workplaces, and all of the states have laws in place that restrict smoking in government buildings with more than 70% prohibiting smoking in government buildings completely.[6]

"Can you talk?"

"Sure, just give me a minute."

Hearing Tom's voice on the other end gives Sherry a momentary rush. Having picked up the phone the moment Pat left her office, Sherry could hardly wait to share. While holding for Tom to return to the line, she smiles to herself, realizing how comfortable she's become, able to call him for just about anything. A moment later he's back.

"So what's up?"

"Pat just was here."

"Which Pat?"

"Pat, your senior partner colleague."

"Oh, really? What did she want?"

"You sound surprised?"

"Well, kind of. I wasn't aware you knew each other. And Pat is not famous for just chatting around."

"You make me laugh. Number one, we didn't just 'chat around.' And number two, we didn't know each other, but now we do."

"Nice. I have a lot of respect for Pat. So how did she end up in your office?"

"That's what I'm trying to tell you—if I may?"

Reacting, Tom softens his tone:

"Of course you may, Sherry. I'm sorry. I guess I was still pissed at the associate I was talking to just before you called. Go ahead."

"Pat came to congratulate me on the Lara Croft initiative—"

"Really…? That's pretty cool."

"—and to share some of her observations: First, she was positively surprised how many people participated in the initiative… She even explicitly complimented me on the smart choice of the award—"

"She really said that?"

"Yes, she did… But even more surprising to her was the fact that it actually worked. For the past few weeks, she has been tracking the time her people left work to see if the buzz about Lara was just a lot of noise or if the initiative is really having an impact. On some of her teams, people were leaving, on average, 2 hours earlier than before. Can you believe that?"

"Of course, I could have told her that without tracking. I have run dozens of such programs with my clients. Believe me, it *does* work."

"Come on, Mister. She is not the only one who is surprised to see it work. I'm surprised, too. It means that people have been voluntarily working longer hours than necessary. That simply goes against common sense."

"All right. What else has she observed?"

"That there are teams out there for which it doesn't work."

"Did she say which ones?"

"No. Even after I pressed her, she wouldn't volunteer any names."

"That's Pat… But I can tell you the ones in my office."

"And I can tell you the ones in my office. But what's

amazing to me, Tom, is how those few teams—and they are clearly in the minority—are able to create an atmosphere that makes *everybody* in the firm willing to work longer hours?"

"Well, if you want to change that, my dear, you first have to expose them as the minority. So far, to most people, I'd say they appear to be the vast majority."

"But how is that possible? Aren't we all supposed to be smart people, who are capable of making independent decisions... I mean, can't we decide when a job is done, when a presentation is good to go... and then just go home?"

"Call it a mix of legacy and human nature. The legacy of working long hours and the human nature of going with the flow. I know it's hard to believe, but even in a high-performing environment like ours people actually choose to go with the flow. After all, it's the easiest way to go, the course of least resistance."

"I see. I guess you're right... and I'm embarrassed to say, I'm one of them."

"Actually, I'd say you *were* one of them... and so was I. But..." Abruptly, out of nowhere, Tom shifts into his best Bob Dylan imitation: "*The times, they are a-changin'...*"

Hearing him, Sherry laughs. Pleased at her reaction, he adds: "I think we are on to something, Sherry, I really do. I can see the story unfolding. Soon it will be time for us to formalize our project."

"I agree... I've already asked an associate to collect some additional data to make our case... And before I forget, Pat also suggested that I reach out to you. She remembered your comments at the meeting and connected the dots."

"Has anybody else?"

"No. Arjun and a few others complemented me on Lara, but didn't make any effort to measure the impact or see the connection."

"Fair enough… And I'm really starting to like Lara."

"I'm glad. But it took you a while!"

"That's me, Sherry. I always need to see the proof myself. Let me know as soon as you have the results from your additional data analyses and we'll discuss it…"

"Sounds good."

"And we also need to plan our next dinner!"

"This time I will come to New York. I just need to wait until Oscar adjusts to his new teacher and his class."

"No hurry, Sherry. I'm enjoying our time just as it is."

In retrospect, changing the standard from smoking to non-smoking doesn't look like such a big deal because intuitively it feels like it was the right thing to do. It almost feels inevitable. We should be able to choose if we are willing to breath secondhand smoke or not, shouldn't we? After all, it's a question of our personal health.

But of course, what looks so intuitive and right today was a tough sell back when the old standard was still firmly entrenched. That's why it's so crucial that we reframe the problem. How we position and sell the new standard is essential to its success. We will never reach the critical mass necessary to effect change unless we have the right incentive that appeals not to the fervent supporters nor to the fervent resisters, but to those in the middle, the undecided ones.

WHAT WE HAVE IN COMMON WITH SMOKERS

Similar to elections, it's neither the loyal Democrats nor the loyal Republicans who make or break a president or governor. Rather, the bulk of campaign time and money is spent on the undecided voters and first-time voters, the voters who can make a difference. Therefore, if we want to be successful in bringing about change, we need to develop a compelling story that will appeal to the undecided mind.

It is important to recognize that being undecided does not mean a person *doesn't* care about the topic. They have simply accepted an arrangement that allows them to exist within the current situation in order to accommodate it. They have developed workarounds to cope with it and are silently accepting the frustrations that come with it (for example, they postpone the morning coffee break until the heavy smokers have left the cafeteria, or they switch their cubicle to sit closer to a window). In fact, they have become so accustomed to the status quo that they don't realize anymore how much they must compromise every day (for instance, scheduling their coffee break around the smokers rather than around their own work routine or choosing the cubicle farthest from the smokers rather than closest to their co-workers). So when confronted with an alternative that offers a completely fresh perspective, their initial reaction is hesitance, even confusion. It will take them a while to understand—and even more importantly—to admit that this alternative is actually what they have secretly always wished for instead of their present compromise. And even after they have figured it out, the cost of change still might appear too great given the investments they have made to cope with the current situation. So they decide to wait and see.

Typically, the undecided ones outnumber the sum total of the supporters and resisters by far. Hence winning the hearts and minds of those people still on the fence becomes crucial for success. The key is to show them their true needs, to make them realize that what you are offering is what they really want. And how do we do that? By reframing the problem, by showing them a new way, a new perspective from which to look at the problem.

This is exactly what the non-smokers did: Instead of looking at smoking as a lifestyle choice, they turned it into a health choice. Under the old standard, smoking was considered cool—by smokers and non-smokers alike. And who wants to be un-cool? But by looking at it from a health perspective, suddenly the question was: Who wants to be unhealthy? The dividing line shifted from life-style to life itself. Suddenly it was no longer a matter of coolness but a matter of health. This completely reset the situation. Significantly, it was the smokers who had to explain why they were willing to live unhealthy lives, rather than the non-smokers having to explain why they were willing to be seen as un-cool. By reframing the problem, the burden of proof had shifted, and the true need—the need for a smoke-free environment—was revealed. Now the door for those who were still undecided was wide open.

Of course, they still had to walk through that door before becoming part of the new, emerging majority. But it was now a question of *when*, no longer *if* they would be supporting the new standard. Once they had realized their true need, it was almost impossible for them to ignore the gap between that need and what the current situation had to offer. Realizing a need, however, doesn't automatically mean one is willing to admit it. Thus the next step—helping them to admit their need—wasn't necessarily easy. Not because they didn't know the answer (of course they wanted to live healthy lives), but because they didn't know how to go about it. Should they really stand up against their own friends who happen to be smokers? And what if they enjoy smoking a cigar from time to time themselves? Should they entirely abandon that habit? What about other equally unhealthy habits like pipe smoking? And more generally, should smoking be banned from all public places? How about workplaces? Should it be banned completely, or would it be sufficient to have dedicated smoking areas and rooms?

Obviously, the ultimate goal of the emerging majority was to create a 100% smoke-free environment for public places as well as workplaces. But there are many different ways to achieve this. And while we will never know if there might have been faster or smarter ways of getting to where we are today, there are two sets of options that any emerging majority has to consider carefully when building towards the critical mass: (1) it can choose between an inclusive versus exclusive solution; and (2) it can choose between a radical versus gradual transformation. The more inclusive the solution, the easier it will be for those who are undecided to support it; and the more gradual the transformation, the easier it will be to accept and eventually join.

Given the existence of secondhand smoke, the first lever was not really an option for the non-smokers. Theoretically, one could have worked towards two separate environments—one for smokers and another for non-smokers—with separate restaurants, hotels, airlines, etc. in order to satisfy both parties' needs. But first, this would not have solved the question of public spaces. And second, given the continually decreasing number of smokers,—such a solution was economically simply unfeasible.

It is, however, important to realize how far an inclusive approach will take us versus an exclusionary one. It's not about appeasing the emerging majority (this is just a side effect). It is about making it easy for those who are undecided to switch sides because they don't have to go *against* anything; they only have to go *for* something. In addition, an inclusive solution makes it also much easier for the next layer of society—the corporate world, schools, and government—to support, or at least not oppose, the new standard, which in turn makes it even easier for the undecided ones to join. That's why an inclusive solution—if feasible—is strongly preferable.

The second lever was successfully applied by the non-smokers—or, depending on whom you ask, enforced by the tobacco lobby. Fact is, that smoking bans were introduced step-by-step, first by having separate areas for smokers, then by having separate rooms for smokers, then introducing complete smoking bans. It helped the undecided business owners, for example, the owners of restaurants, to realize that they could still make money, maybe even more, by limiting the smokers' freedom. And it helped the undecided buyers of those services, for example, the guests of those restaurants, to realize how big of an improvement it made to have less smoke in the air, not to mention what a difference it would make to have no smoke in the air.

But more importantly, introducing a new standard step-by-step will help the undecided ones to recognize that an increasing number of their peers share the same need, a need that they previously hadn't even realized they held in common. And the more peers they observe embracing that same need, the more comfortable they will be admitting to it themselves. Which also explains why imposing a new standard on those who are undecided can have the exact opposite effect resulting in less, not more support for the cause, which brings us to the final point: The role of governmental support.

Of course, government can speed up the process by legally requiring the new standard be introduced top-down. However, as long as the new, emerging majority has not done its homework to reach the critical mass necessary to establish the new standard, the old majority will find creative ways to quietly continue living by their old standard. Outsourcing the problem to the government may seem like an attractive option. But it will never address the root cause of the problem because at the root of any problem is our very own behavior and attitudes, which brings us back to Einstein who said that you cannot solve a problem with the same mind-set that created it.

6

What We Really Want (But Are Afraid to Ask For)

When Tom's cell phone rings, he checks the screen, pleased to see Sherry's name. Pressing "accept," he can barely wait to tell her the news.

"Sherry, I'm glad you called. I've signed us up to present our project at the next senior partners meeting. You will need to come to New York. Do you have time to connect later tonight?"

"That's great! You really want me to be there?"

"Of course, this is *our* project!"

"Sure. I will call you once Oscar is asleep."

It is still a month to go until the next senior partners meeting, but Tom wants to come up with a plan, and he wants to hear Sherry's voice anyway. Of course, tonight it takes Oscar extra long to fall asleep—as if he somehow senses mommy's urge to call Tom. When he finally nods off, Sherry quietly slips from the room. Picking up the phone, she dials Tom's number:

"Hi Tom, good evening. Sorry, it took me a while."

"No problem, it's just good to hear your voice. How have you been? How was your day?"

"Fine. Busy. Few client meetings in the morning, a big team meeting in the early afternoon, and then a play date after school."

"I've got to admire you, Sherry. You really seem to be able to combine both... to 'have it all,' as they say."

"Yes—sometimes more successfully than others, but generally it seems to work. The trick is simple: Keeping both my work life and home life as part of the same agenda. To me there aren't two things, only one... not sure I'm making sense."

"I think what you are saying is not wrong. It should be one thing, one sphere. But you know, I'm coming at it from exactly the opposite direction. I used to, and still do, completely separate work and home into two spheres... which is—now that I think about it—pretty artificial."

"But easy."

"Very easy indeed... Can I ask you a question, Sherry?"

"Of course, anytime."

"You mentioned a play date. What exactly do you do at a 'play date'? I mean, it sounds extremely boring. If I imagine you running a client meeting versus running a play date—they seem totally different. "

"Of course. And it is quite different. The same way it's

different to talk to a CEO versus interview a undergrad for an internship."

"I'm not sure I follow."

"What I'm trying to say is that even within our work sphere the things we do are quite different. To me, having a play date is just another part of my job… and play dates are not boring at all. I love to observe the way my little boy interacts with others—how he enjoys himself, how proud of himself he is when he does something new… even how he struggles."

"But do you really need a play date to observe those things?"

"I do. The difference is that when I set up a play date, I make a conscious decision to dedicate time to my son, not just to have him around. It's a big difference, Tom."

"If you say so."

"And of course I always try to pick parents with whom I'm interested in spending some time as well. You can learn a lot from other parents… and sometimes it gives you an opportunity to share your own concerns. Again, very similar to work—think of all the chit-chat that happens before and after (and even during) the meetings. It's often about sharing our concerns, isn't it?"

"So what did you learn today, Sherry…? I don't mean to pry, but it all sounds a little too much of a fairytale to me."

"Today was actually quite interesting. We talked about some after school activities—things our kids have been doing outside of school. And he had quite an interesting proposal for how we—"

"He? You had a play date with a guy?"

"Yes, the father of the other boy—a fine guy. He is an executive at one of the big brokerage firms in the city…"

Sensing an uncomfortable silence on the other end of the line, Sherry hesitates.

"Tom…?"

"Yes, I'm here… Just caught me off guard."

"Are you jealous?"

"Yes…" Catching himself, Tom quickly attempts to clarify. "No… That's not the point… I simply never considered anyone other than mothers as having play dates for their kids. It just never occurred to me."

"Fair enough. I hope it does now. If you think about it, it's the same as women participating business meetings, just the other way around."

"I get it, Sherry. Good point. Thank you…" Then he adds: "But of course, business meetings don't happen at home, so at least there are some sort of formal rules of engagement."

"Now you're making me laugh, Tom."

"Why? I don't like strange men visiting you in your apartment. What's wrong with that?"

"He is not a stranger, Tom… And if your worry is that those men would try to jump me… they can just as easily jump me in the office. Actually, it's much easier in the office, because there are no kids around!"

"Why you always have to be so radical, Sherry?"

"Because otherwise you don't get the point, Tom."

Stung, Tom says nothing. The silence lengthens. It's

Sherry who finally speaks again, attempting to tactfully change the subject.

"Why don't we talk about our presentation to the senior partners? It becomes even more relevant seeing how deeply ingrained these beliefs still are."

"No thank you, Sherry… I just need some time. And please don't get me wrong this time. I'm not saying that I disagree. I'm just not ready yet."

"All right, Tom, understood… It's a tough problem. Which is why we seem to be having such a hard time solving it. We—the society, I mean. And that's why I'm so excited to work with you on this project."

"I know you are. So am I. You are very sweet, Sherry. We'll speak again soon. Good night."

"Good night."

Now it's our turn. Now it's up to us to figure out how to create the critical mass to establish a new standard, a standard that doesn't induce guilt, a standard that will finally allow us to have it all. Today's standard is build on the assumption that the majority of men want to be the sole breadwinner and that the majority of women want to be the sole caregiver. Hence women are the minority at work and men are the minority at home. But is this really true or are we perceiving majorities that actually don't exist?

Remember, smoking used to stand for coolness, which turned smokers into the perceived majority, despite being in the numerical minority. Maybe being the sole breadwinner stands for success, even for true masculinity. And maybe

WHAT WE REALLY WANT (BUT ARE AFRAID TO ASK FOR)

being the sole caregiver stands for love—love for our kids, love for our husband (by enabling his success)—even for true femininity. Maybe it's the air of success and the air of love that is distorting our perception of who is in the majority and who is in the minority? Maybe the majority of men do *not* want to be the sole breadwinner and maybe the majority of women do *not* want to be the sole caregiver—*if* they had a choice. But they don't. Men are either successful breadwinners—or labeled as unsuccessful wimps. And women are either loving caretakers—or labeled as unloving careerist? Now which man wants to be perceived as unsuccessful? And which woman wants to be perceived as unloving? No one.

That's exactly the situation the non-smokers found themselves in when they started their campaign—nobody wanted to be un-cool. But everyone—or at least the majority—wanted to be healthy. So they reframed the problem accordingly. Today's parents are in a similar situation. Nobody wants to be unsuccessful or unloving. But what if we asked them: Do you want to be happy? In other words: Do you want to live the way *you* want, or the way it is expected of you? Do you want to choose or to be told what to do? In the same way non-smokers turned a matter of coolness into a matter of health, parents could turn a matter of gender into a matter of preferences. And their preferences are quite clear, if we take the time to ask:[1]

"My ideal situation would be…	Moms	Dads
to stay at home with the kids."	19%	16%
to take care of the kids while having a career."	53%	46%
to focus on my career."	27%	38%

Surprised? Yes and no. Yes, because it goes against what conventional wisdom would tell us to expect. No, if we consider what we learned in the previous chapters. First, that the similarities between men and women outnumber the differences between them by far. So it shouldn't come as a surprise that this also holds true for their lifestyle choices. Second, that guilt makes us suppress our preferences, our true needs. Hence it was almost impossible to even know the true needs of the other parents around us. But by reframing the problem from a gender into a lifestyle question, we are able to unveil the parents' true needs. And with their true needs on the table, the majorities look suddenly quite different. Because if we partner those 53% of moms who want to combine family and career with those 46% of dads who want the same, we will have created the critical mass to build a new majority at home as well as at work. Done.

"Hi, it's me. Can you please call me back? I had a quite unpleasant encounter with Valerie."

Sherry tries to call Tom right after her exchange with Valerie, but she only gets his Voicemail. Tom picks up her message but doesn't get a chance to call Sherry back until the late afternoon:

"Hi… Tell me what happened."

"Ah, I just had this strange, kind of nasty conversation with

Valerie... in fact, it wasn't really a conversation, it was more like a rant."

"What did she say? And where did you meet her?"

"She was in Chicago for some client meetings and came to my office."

"Oh, so she really made an effort to seek you out... Seems like you're becoming quite popular."

"I think it's more Lara Croft than me. But yes, it felt like she was probing the waters... fishing for what might be next."

"Of course. She is probably getting nervous."

"It actually was quite bizarre, now that I think about it. For example, she didn't mention the Women's Initiative, which seemed very unusual because typically she never misses a chance to promote it... and remind you that she was the one who initiated it. Instead, she tried to make fun of Lara, like she was ridiculing the whole idea."

"Give me an example."

"She was saying things like, 'Oh, I wonder who the boob was who came up with that Lara Croft idea?' or 'At least now that we have Lara Croft, we know the men will be sure to keep abreast of who's working long hours.'"

Tom starts laughing:

"Wow, that's really to the point, I must say."

"True. But it's not funny, Tom. Why are you laughing?"

"Come on, Sherry, you can't let her get to you. You didn't expect everyone to be supportive?"

"But she is a women! She keeps preaching flexible work hours and all the other goodies that go with the Women's

Initiative. But how can you be flexible if you insist on working long hours at the same time?"

"It's not that she insists on long work hours, Sherry, she just doesn't know how to cut back."

"Bullshit, Tom. She believes that in order to be successful—woman or man—you need to work long hours… And so does the rest of the firm. Period."

"Calm down, Sherry. Of course there is this strong belief that in order to be successful at our firm you have to put in the hours. And *because* this belief is so ingrained, we need to tackle the problem from a different angle—and that's exactly what you and I have been doing. That's why I offered to work with you on this project in the first place. Because I really saw an opportunity to change things for the better. I would have never signed up for anything less. That's not me."

Reassured by the conviction in Tom's voice, Sherry starts to calm down.

"Remember how we said that we have to do things differently in order to make people see and listen?"

"Of course…"

"So please don't forget that. It's crucial that we stick to the script."

"But exactly what is our 'script,' Tom?"

"Everything we've been working on. This is what we have so far: First, we made them see that many of us—dads as well as moms—want more personal time… and more predictability. Second, we made them see how much time we waste on a daily basis. So we've established that there *is* clearly room for improvement. Now we have to show them how to improve and we're done. That's our script."

"Hmmm... sounds a little too simple to me."

"The simplest stories are the best, Sherry. Why do you want to complicate something that is not complicated at all?"

"Because when the problem seems so hard to solve, it usually means that it is complicated."

"But we've already established that it's not."

"I know, I know."

"So you agree... or not?" Sensing Sherry hesitate, Tom continues: "Take Valerie, for example: We will show her how to work smarter instead of longer. If she is serious about her claims, she will jump on it and leverage the extra time to have it all. Otherwise, we can't help her."

Sherry starts to laugh:

"I agree...!"

"I'm serious, Sherry. That's it. And I would not do any more than that."

"Well, it's just a little hard to believe that nobody at this firm but us has figured out how to work smarter."

"Don't underestimate how difficult it is. The higher up in the hierarchy you go, the more challenging it becomes. Working smarter requires making decisions on your own and trusting people on your team to also make smart decisions on their own."

"But that takes trust—and you can't teach trust!"

"True, but you can teach a process by which to build trust."

"Then I guess I'm going to learn something, too."

"I promise you, Sherry, you will. But for now let's focus on the storyline for the meeting. I liked the data your associate gathered, but ideally we need to show an even stronger correlation between the way poor working styles at the top waste time across the entire hierarchy."

"Yes, I was thinking the same thing. Let me do a little more research and I will get back to you!"

Unfortunately, recognizing our needs doesn't automatically mean that we admit them. After years of living within the guilt-inducing framework of female caregivers and male breadwinners, this will not be easy. Because it is one thing to define our needs within the parameters determined by society (which can provide a good excuse to ignore or hide our true needs), and it is a completely different thing to turn inwards and attempt to identify our own true needs without any outside guidance or framework. To then disclose them—to justify them—to our spouse, to our boss, to our peers is exceptionally difficult.

This is particularly true for a topic that touches some of the most private and personal elements of our lives—our unconditional love for our children, our romanticized ideal of a happy family, and our desire for success. Any criticism of how we raise our kids, how we envision and manage our family life, and how we pursue our career, we readily interpret as a personal provocation, as an intrusion into our private sphere. And any compromises we are forced to make, we readily perceive as a personal failure. As a result, instinctively, we avoid these topics. And if we are forced to talk about it, we become protective and defensive.

WHAT WE REALLY WANT (BUT ARE AFRAID TO ASK FOR)

Contrary to the question of smoking, however, which is first and foremost an individual, simple yes-or-no decision, the question of how to run our household is both a joint decision and a rather complex one. So it will be hard to make that decision without discussing it with our spouse, without revealing our true needs, and without the readiness to make some compromises. The good news, however, is that those compromises will be based on a conscious decision rather than being imposed by guilt; and hence they will no longer feel like trade-offs, but rather like a deal, a deal between us and our spouses. But to unlock this reward we have to start talking. And this will be by far the biggest obstacle to winning the hearts and minds of those who are still undecided.

Luckily, we can make full use of the two levers in our toolbox to influence the ease and pace of the transformation: First, we can offer a completely inclusive solution because there is no right or wrong way when it comes to parenting, because there is no single way of running a household, and because there is no one path to a successful career. Rather, each set of parents will have to define their own way of parenting and running their own household to reflect the specific needs of their family. And each set of parents must define and align the type of careers they want, reflecting the specific needs of each of them. Of course, the kids have to be safe and healthy; and of course, the family has to have enough money to live on. But there is no universal definition of "safe," "healthy," or "how much money is enough." Rather, each family will have to arrive at its own definition. So basically what we are attempting to do is provide true choice for everyone: Let the pure breadwinners and caregivers—male and female—do their thing, if this is really what they want to do. And if they want to join the working parents at a later stage, they are more than welcome to do so.

Second, we can offer an individualized and gradual transformation. In fact, given the sensitivity and complexity of the topic, that's the only way to go. Obviously, we can't proceed by space as the non-smokers did, first introducing smoke-free areas, then smoke-free rooms, ultimately leading to complete indoor smoking bans. Rather, it will be by circle of influence. Think of a circle with you in the center. Then a bigger circle around the first circle, then a still bigger circle around the second circle, and so forth. Each circle represents an additional sphere of influence. First, it will just be us. We have to recognize our true needs. It is not even necessary to admit them yet. Just quietly observe ourselves, our environment, and what we think, how we behave. Then comes the second circle, our spouse. That's when the talking starts, finding a way to share, admit our needs, and compare notes. The third circle might be our mommy friends, or our buddies, or the other parents at school, or our own mom, or mother-in-law. With each circle we are broadening our sphere of influence to establish the new standard, one undecided parent at a time.

The key to creating the critical mass is to clearly outline the path to success: We must show that it *is* possible to get what we really want as long as we take the time to understand what it will take us to get there. Today, we simply don't know

WHAT WE REALLY WANT (BUT ARE AFRAID TO ASK FOR)

how to go about it, how to talk about it, how to bring things up and make things happen. And we will not learn how to do all this by looking at idealized role models. It won't help us to know how others have done it because each situation is unique and highly personal. Thus, in order to find our way, we will need a clearly structured yet flexible process that will allow each of us to embrace and adapt it to our specific situation. The bottom line: This is about making it *your* story—the story of you and your spouse having it all.

PART 3

How Tom and Sherry Make It Happen: The power of seeing the obvious

7

If You Want Something, Say So...

"Are you ready, my dear?"

Tom is standing at the door of the guest office that Sherry has been using for the day. She is almost ready to go, glancing over the desk to make sure she hasn't forgotten anything while slipping into her jacket. Then she looks at Tom with a smile, her eyes sparkling:

"Yes, I am."

"You look happy."

"I *am* happy. I really enjoyed today's discussion with the senior partners. And now I'm looking forward to dinner with you."

"Excellent. Because I picked the perfect restaurant."

"I'm sure you did. And I am actually starving."

Tom and Sherry decide to walk the few blocks to the restaurant.

"So what did you enjoy most about the discussion today, Sherry?"

"Oh, that's easy. The fact that they listened... they really became fully engaged—not all of them, but we definitely had everyone's attention."

"That's mostly thanks to you. The data you and your team collected, and the way you presented it really took them off guard."

"My guess is they've never been so exposed before, at least not in those 'hidden' dimensions such as how well they scope or manage their projects."

"Absolutely! My favorite slide is still the one with the 'Notorious Over-deliverers'!"

Suppressing a smile, Sherry is pleased. "Good thing we didn't put any names on it!"

"I think it was less about the names—people know who they are—than it is about how great the differences between individual partners actually are."

"True... And that it affects the teams who are working for them... But most importantly, by over-delivering that they fail to make a serious contribution to our bottom line."

"Of course not, how can they? To over-deliver, by definition, means that you have negotiated a bad deal... It was *so* beautiful the way you linked the 'cost' of the people who had left the firm to the 'balance sheet' of each partner who had contributed to their leaving."

"It was a little nasty but effective. And it nicely paved the way for our core message: That the measures we are currently employing to manage retention have zero impact—or even worse, a negative impact."

"I have to admit that I'm still surprised myself at the data. I mean every one of those measures cost us serious time and money. But we clearly had no clue who was actually making use of them—people who leave the firm anyway!"

"And it's not only women!"

"I know, I know… that was critical. And the way you managed to push back when they attempted to pin it on gender. Very nicely finessed. My compliments!"

"You mean the 'Band-Aids'…?"

"Yes, exactly."

"But it's true. All we are doing is putting Band-Aids on serious wounds instead of treating them. That's how we end up with all those useless, counter-productive policies—without ever touching the real problem: The inefficient way we work."

"Of course, it's true, Sherry. And I think Pat did a fine job summarizing the point when she said that our current way of working is simply outdated."

"Oh my gosh, yes. I got goose bumps when she said it! We couldn't have said it better!"

Tom stops walking and puts his arm around Sherry, pulling her close:

"And you, my sweet lady… *you* give me goose bumps!"

He kisses her, first softly, then passionately—completely oblivious to the people passing by on the sidewalk around them. Sherry doesn't have time to be surprised. She is simply lost in the moment, her body melting into his as he draws her to him. When he finally speaks, his voice is just above a whisper:

"I hope you enjoyed your *first* kiss, Madame!"

"Absolutely… and definitely worth the wait," she whispers back.

Tom takes Sherry's hand and they walk the last two blocks to the restaurant in silence, enjoying the delicate intimacy of just holding each other's hand.

Now that we understand how majorities are built and how those who are undecided can be won over, we must go and actually *do* it. There is no secret to success, no magic potion, but a process that must be followed. As a matter of fact, choosing the right process *will* make the difference. To illustrate just how big of a difference it can make to follow the right process, consider the following tale.[1]

Once upon a time, there was a young engineer who was eager to put the ailing business of his uncle back on track. To tell the truth, the business had never been on track. But the young engineer was determined to make it work, and he lacked neither ability nor ambition to do so. And off he went on an extended trip overseas to visit and carefully analyze one of the industry's leaders and, as it would turn out, a major competitor-to-be. In his letter back to corporate headquarters, he enthusiastically reported that there was quite some room for improvement, which he believed could be leveraged to create a competitive advantage. This was in spring of 1950. The young engineer was Eiji Toyoda of

Toyota, and the competitor he visited was the Ford Motor Company in Detroit.

At that time, Ford, jointly with General Motors and Chrysler, were the uncontested leaders of the auto industry. The Big Three or Detroit Three, as they were called, had made the U.S. the leading automobile manufacturer in the world at the time, responsible for 95% of the car sales in the U.S.[2]

This market dominance was the result of mass production, a process invented by Henry Ford. Ford's revolutionary idea: To make an automobile that a man working on the production line could afford to own. The key behind its success was standardization. Ford's method churned out huge volumes of standardized products—automobiles: one model, one color—allowing for lowest possible production cost. All elements of the manufacturing process were optimized towards that goal: Each machine was designed to produce exactly one part of the car. Each worker was trained to perform exactly one task of the workflow. And rigid procedures were put in place to keep machines and workers in sync at every point along the assembly line. Ford's approach had revolutionized manufacturing and made America a dominant force throughout the world.

Eiji was, of course, very impressed by this carefully designed process capable of producing more cars *in a single day* than his uncle had ever produced. But while observing the workers at their workstations, something caught his eye: When a worker found a defective part, he immediately put the piece in a designated storage area right behind him and continued with a new piece, making sure not to disrupt the flow of the production line. Later on, another worker would come by to pick up the defective piece and bring it over to a designated repair area. There, workers from the repair department would try to repair the defective piece without any information as to what might have caused the defect. Maybe the machine hadn't worked properly? Maybe the worker had made a mistake? Or maybe the material was already damaged before it arrived at the workstation? When a worker piled up too many defective pieces, the quality control department would get involved. They would send a quality control specialist to oversee the underperforming worker, despite the fact that no one had taken the time to identify the source of the defects. Nonetheless, the worker would either improve or be replaced.

Why was this observation so important? It made Eiji realize that Ford's process only worked as long as there were no defects. Thus, the system was highly vulnerable to any sort of disruption. Disruptions were the Achilles heel of mass production. But as he knew too well from his own experience back in Japan, disruptions were part of the daily manufacturing routine. No wonder Ford had organized the entire process around managing these disruptions. In doing so, he had built buffers along the entire production line. This meant buying extra supplies to provide enough new pieces for its workers at their workstations. This, in turn, required extra space to store both the extra supplies as well as the defective parts coming back from the workstations. And finally Ford was forced to hire extra workers to manage and control all of this. Each of these buffers added extra cost to every single car Ford produced. Having identified this flaw in the system, Eiji was sure Toyota could do better than this. With that in mind, he traveled home.

"Call me."

Tom is in meetings all afternoon. But this is important enough for him to briefly step out to take her call as soon as Sherry becomes available. He hasn't seen this coming, and he wants to tell her before somebody else does. The moment his cell phone begins to vibrate, he excuses himself and slips into the hallway to answer it:

"Sherry? Hi! … Can't talk long. I have to jump back into my meeting, but you won't believe what happened this morning. We had our quarterly budget meeting—the one where we really go through the numbers…"

"You're on the Budget Committee…? You never mentioned it."

"Just never came up… sorry. In any case, for the next quarter there were two of those women-something workshops in the budget. So out of the blue, John—"

"John…?" Reacting, Sherry can barely conceal the surprise in her voice, "You mean… the big boss?"

"Yes, John, the big boss, raises the question: Do we still need those workshops given the presentation they had heard the day before."

"The presentation…? He was referring to us?"

"Yep… Of course, the decision hasn't been made yet. But John made it quite clear that he has no intention in adding any more workshops or training sessions for any sort of integration or retention purposes. On the contrary, he thinks we should seriously review all our existing policies and come up with a more effective approach. He even referred to your Band-Aid analogy!"

"Oh, wow…"

"So basically, what it means is that there is an immediate freeze on all such workshops—with the exception of those that have already sent out invitations—and at the next national partner meeting, we will vote on it."

"What you mean we will vote? On what?"

"On how we want to improve our retention—through initiatives and workshops or through changing our way of working."

"You mean either-or?"

"Yes, either-or. And since the Women's Initiative is one of the bigger budget items—I hate to say—it kind of boils down to Lara versus Women."

"Oops."

"Yes, oops. That's why I wanted to make sure you heard it from me first."

"Thank you. This is a little unexpected."

"Well, I should have seen it coming. That's what usually happens once you create transparency."

"What usually happens?"

"People start taking action, often almost blindly because the solution suddenly seems so obvious, and they don't want to be seen as the ones who have missed out on it."

"But that's the whole purpose of this exercise, no? Identify the problem."

"Of course. I guess John was just a little faster than I expected... which is good... But to be honest, he isn't completely there yet."

"What makes you say that?"

"Because he made comments like: 'The concept is good, but Tom, I'm holding you responsible for making certain there's no loss in productivity. This new approach can't become an excuse for everyone suddenly leaving at 6 p.m. without having their work done.'"

"And what did you say?"

"That once we learn to work more efficiently, productivity will be up, not down. People should want to leave by 6 p.m. But it will be because their work is done."

"I'm sure you are right, Tom. Lara gave us a taste for it. But it is amazing how we fail to trust our own employees to do what's right given how much time we invest in testing their 'attitude' and 'values' during the interview process."

"Trust is not easy, Sherry, particularly if the way you work doesn't support it. But we'll get there, I'm positive. We just have to provide the right motivation. Given the fatigue around the Women's Initiative, some people, including John, are a little too eager to find an excuse to scale the whole program back."

"That's exactly what I'm worried about, Tom. I think it's time to talk to Valerie."

"Good idea... As for the rest, we just let the message sink in a little longer and then come up with concrete approach—just as I had originally planned. I guess I underestimated how much of an impact our message was going to have."

"You underestimated how sensitive the topic is, Tom."

"Yes I did… and something else, Sherry… "

"What's that…?"

"I also underestimated how much I miss those kisses."

Caught completely by surprise, Sherry doesn't know how to respond.

"The ones I got *after* dinner!"

Remembering the moment they shared, she feels a chill.

"Sherry?"

Lowering her voice, she whispers into the phone: "I'm in the office, Tom."

"So?"

"Sometimes you are impossible."

"But teasing you is so much fun."

"So it would seem."

"And you can't escape any longer—because you are now officially working with me."

Sherry blushes, Tom's comment reminds her of his firm grip when he was kissing her.

"Tom, please… I have to go."

But Tom isn't listening: "But that's exactly how you like it, isn't it?"

"I'm hanging up now…"

"Where do you have to rush to?"

"Nowhere… But if it would make you feel better, I can make up something."

"Nasty woman. I love when you get annoyed—makes you

IF YOU WANT SOMETHING, SAY SO...

even more sexy. Run wherever you want, my lady,—just know I'm going to catch you."

Back home, Eiji suggested—for primarily domestic reasons—that Toyota should not replicate mass production and try to produce an even cheaper car. Rather, it should try to produce a *better* car at the same price, correcting the weaknesses he had observed in Detroit. And that's exactly what they did. Jointly with Taiichi Ohno, a one-in-a-kind engineer, they radically redesigned the production process to offer a car that customers would prefer, but could still afford. As a result, customers were suddenly able to choose from a variety of car models and colors without paying much more. How was this possible? By making the production line less vulnerable to disruptions, and hence no longer needing all those expensive buffers. How did Toyota do that? By creating transparency. Transparency became the cornerstone of the Toyota production line.

Let's take a closer look how this new approach would play out in a situation similar to the one that caught Eiji's eye during his visit to Ford. When a worker on the assembly line found a defective part at Toyota, the issue was addressed immediately. If necessary, the production line was stopped—an absolute no-go at Ford. Then proceeding jointly with his colleagues, the worker would analyze the issue to understand the source of the defect. Was it the machine that malfunctioned? Or had the worker, himself, made a mistake (which was perfectly acceptable as long as he learned from it)? Or perhaps the material itself was defective?

Let's assume they concluded that the material was defective. The next step would be to understand why. If, in looking deeper, it turned out that the manufacturing process, itself, had created the defect, they would analyze the process, identify the root cause, and correct it accordingly. If the defect was traced to the supplier, the supervisor would immediately reach out to the supplier and ask him to solve the problem. And since each worker along the production line had been trained to perform multiple tasks, they were able to substitute for each other while working to solve the problem. Once it was solved, or—if the problem was too complex to be solved immediately—once a temporary solution was in place, the workers went back to their regular tasks.

By creating full transparency from the moment the defect was discovered, the team was able to figure out the root cause and take appropriate measures without the need for extra supplies, extra space, or extra workers. Of course, the disruption of the production lasted a little longer than the one that Eiji observed in Detroit. But while at Ford the same disruption would happen over and over again until it was eliminated, at Toyota every disruption only happened once. Hence the total disruption time was much shorter.

The entire system at Toyota was (and still is) designed to foster transparency: Instead of single-purpose machines, it employs highly flexible machines that can be easily understood and adapted by the workers. Instead of narrowly trained, typically unskilled workers, it relies on a skilled, well-trained workforce, who are capable of performing multiple tasks and are empowered to make decisions. And instead of

IF YOU WANT SOMETHING, SAY SO...

rigid procedures, it has flexible procedures in place that can easily be adjusted by the workers if need be. But the biggest difference is in the attitude, the mindset of each worker, each employee—from the very bottom to the top of the pyramid: Instead of control fostering a culture of fear and constant uncertainty, Toyota built on trust, fostering a culture of transparency and problem solving. As a result, instead of blindly surrendering to the status quo, Toyota was driven to relentlessly improve their product. This in turn translated into a superior automobile with an international reputation for outstanding quality.

Let me end the story by fast forwarding to the 1980s. By then Japan had surpassed the U.S. as the leading automobile manufacturer in the world and Japanese carmakers commanded a 20% market share in the U.S.[3] Now it was the U.S. producers who visited the Japanese plants. On their visit to Toyota's first plant on American soil, a manager insisted that "secret repair areas and secret inventories had to exist behind the plant, because he hadn't seen enough of either for a 'real' plant."[4] And another manager left wondering what all the fuss was about: "They build cars just like we do."

He was absolutely right with respect to the end product as such, both produced cars. But he completely underestimated the impact of the process on the bottom line: To assemble a car, Toyota needed half the space that GM needed, had one third of the defects that GM had, and—most impressively—assembled two cars in the time that GM assembled one.[5]

This shows how Toyota was able to have it all, how it

was able to offer a better car *and* at a competitive price: by eliminating waste on a grand scale. Nobody in American automobile manufacturing could have imagined that such a vast improvement was even possible. Instead, the American mind-set was stuck in the belief that a better car—by definition—comes at the trade-off of higher cost, because better quality can only be achieved through greater control. By radically rethinking how to work, however, Toyota proved that the opposite was true, that too much control makes the production process *more* vulnerable to disruptions, not less. Hence, by replacing control with trust, it was able to minimize disruptions. And by minimizing disruptions, it was able to eliminate waste on that grand scale. "Having it all" was suddenly no longer an abstract concept. Toyota had proven that it was possible.

Unsurprisingly, what Toyota pioneered in automobile production quickly became the gold standard for all industries. Who doesn't want to have it all? Today, banks, hospitals, even non-profits such as the Food Bank for New York City are run the Toyota way.[6] Guess who's next?

"Cheers…"

Sherry raises her glass to Valerie, who smiles as she replies:

"Indeed… Thanks for coming my way."

Sipping white wine, Sherry and Valerie are sitting in the lounge of the hotel off Rush Street that Valerie prefers staying at when in Chicago. Having made the extra effort to accommodate Valerie's schedule, Sherry intentionally set the meeting here:

"I appreciate you taking the time... I'm glad we're finally getting a chance to catch up."

"Same here. I was wondering when you were going to reach out. I've been thinking about it a lot."

"About what exactly, Val?"

"Well, first about the Lara Croft initiative. Then about this... I'm not sure what to call it—the 'Work-Different Initiative'...?"

"We still need to come up with a proper name. It all developed a little faster than expected. We wanted to test the idea before working out all the details, including the name."

"But what I don't understand is why you guys came up with it at all? I mean, what's the purpose of it? And why—if I may ask—did you never consult with me?"

"Why...? To answer your first question: Because we are frustrated with where we are as a company today. Tom is frustrated because he is loosing one good guy after another, guys in whom he has invested a lot of time and energy in training. And even more frustrating, they don't leave because they have been lured away by some competing company, but for some sort of work-life balance that Tom doesn't understand. And I—to tell you the truth—am frustrated by having to participate in one women's workshop after another without seeing any meaningful change."

"Why didn't you tell me you felt this way before?"

"I did. Remember...? I made a number of proposals on how to change our messaging towards the rest of the company, even how to open up these workshops to men."

"Of course, I remember. And I will give you the same

answers today that I gave you then: Number one, I don't think we should hide what we want by altering our message; and number two, I don't believe we should share our ideas with those who fail to appreciate them."

"Meaning men."

"Exactly."

"Val, it has nothing to do with hiding what we want. I simply don't believe that it's only women who want this. That's why I wanted to change our message. Many men *are* interested in our ideas, but because of the way we present what we are trying to accomplish, they don't dare to say so."

"You are going to have to show me these men, Sherry. Because I don't believe it. As for our message, it's critical that it remains exactly as is. Otherwise, we would have even fewer women at this firm than we do now."

"I'm not sure about that, Val. I'm sorry to be so blunt, but I looked at the numbers and they tell a different story. We might be getting a few more female analysts. But not any more than other firms. And women are leaving at a faster rate than they used to, which makes our promotion pipeline look worse, not better."

"Don't you think you are being a little unfair, Sherry? A little impatient? Things like this take time."

"I disagree, Val. I think we are working on the wrong problem… And maybe we just have to agree to disagree because I can't offer anything but the facts—the ones I just mentioned and the facts Tom and I presented the other day."

Valerie frowns. Unable to offer a rebuttal, she says nothing.

IF YOU WANT SOMETHING, SAY SO...

"But you had another question, right? Why didn't I consult with you?"

"Yes, why didn't you?"

"Because I don't believe in gender differences. The problem I'm trying to solve has nothing to do with gender."

"Excuse me? You think men and women are all the same?"

"I think there are as many different men out there as there are different women."

"Then how do you explain why fewer women get promoted, despite having equal or better evaluations?"

"They don't, Val. The ones who are good enough and who actively seek to move up get promoted. Otherwise, you and I wouldn't be where we are. Of course, there are always borderline cases, but that's no different for men—just nobody talks about them."

"Then why do the majority of women leave shortly before or after they have children?"

"That's exactly the point! It's about having kids, not about gender."

"But kids are directly related to women, Sherry! Men don't leave because they have babies. Only women do. In what La-La Land are you living?"

"What you're talking about is the general perception, Val. And it's up to us to decide how we want to perceive it."

"Well, the fact is that the majority of people in this firm perceive it the way I do. Period."

"I couldn't agree more. The difference between you and me is how we go about trying to change that perception. See,

Val, I don't believe that you can change someone's perception just by telling him or her to do so."

"And exactly what do you propose?"

"I believe that you can change someone's perception by creating opportunities to behave, to live, to work differently—in line with the new perception that it is okay for everyone to have kids, not only for women."

"And you really believe people will change their behavior just because you provide the opportunity to do so?"

"Opportunity is what it's really all about, Val. Confronted with little or no opportunity to change, the majority won't move despite their desire to do so. And if they—after being given the opportunity—still don't move, then there seems to be no desire for change."

"And as a result, no space in the promotion pipeline for women—is that what you are saying, Sherry?"

"No. I am saying we need to make space for anyone who wants to have kids *and* spend time with them—independent of gender."

"I wish you were right, Sherry."

"I know I am. But I need your help to create that opportunity for everyone—men and women alike—to break down the old self-imposed barriers that prevent us from being the best we can be… from having it all."

As Sherry's words hit home, Valerie frowns.

"Let me think about it, Sherry… Let me think about it some more." Then raising her glass once more, she smiles. "To creating the opportunity…!"

Once Sherry is home from her drinks with Valerie, she texts Tom:
"Had tough but good conversation with Valerie. After she has time to seriously consider our proposal, I think she will come on board!"

The way we currently run our households is strongly reminiscent of the U.S. automobile manufacturers in the 1950s. Of course, our product is not a car but a household. And the key to success is not standardization, but specialization. All elements of the household are optimized towards that goal. Each household has two specialized roles: the Breadwinner for work and the Caregiver for home. Each one of us is assigned to his or her respective role the day we are born. And we are provided with a clear path for specialization, the pink and the blue pipelines, to keep us in sync with our roles at every point along the life cycle (e.g. by suggesting what to study, when to get engaged, married and have kids, and what salary to aim for at what age.)

In the post-war years, when men were generally better educated and had higher earning prospects, this high level of specialization must have looked like a smart idea. But as we all know, society has moved on. Today, women are as equally qualified as men to have a career, and men are as equally (un)prepared as women to be a parent. Yet somehow, despite our best intentions, we find ourselves unable to reach our ultimate goals: Women have entered the Breadwinner world, but rarely make it to the top; and men have entered Caregiver land, but rarely reach the heart of the matter.

The reason for those difficulties lies with the way we organize our households by gender specialization. Similar to the U.S. car makers whose highly standardized processes worked well as long as there were no disruptions, our highly specialized households worked well as long as every woman wanted to be the sole caregiver and every man wanted to be the sole breadwinner. However, once moms started climbing the career ladder, and dads started questioning their role as purely Sunday dads, this high level of specialization became a problem. By definition, specialization doesn't offer much flexibility. Hence, either parents must stick with their specialized role or feel guilty every time they deviate from it. And because we are not male and female robots, but rather human beings, each with a unique set of skills and preferences, guilt has become a daily threat. In fact, guilt has become for us the equivalent to the disruptions that beset the U.S. automakers: Our Achilles heel. And just as the U.S. car manufacturers wasted extra supplies, extra space, and extra workers to manage disruptions, we are wasting extra time and extra energy to manage our guilt—every single day. Similarly, while U.S. automakers were stuck in the belief that producing a better car demanded a trade-off of higher cost, we believe that having it all requires a trade-off of surrendering more of our time. But because every day has only 24 hours, we conclude that having it all is impossible.

Now if Toyota was able to turn this traditional approach of the U.S. carmakers upside down by radically rethinking the way work was performed, we should be able to do the same with our households. We should be able to turn our traditional belief upside down by radically rethinking how we run our household. Does a household need to have two spheres…? Or more…? Or less? Do we allocate responsibilities per sphere…? Per activity…? Or on demand? And do we allocate them by gender or by individual skills and preferences?

Think about how Toyota did it. First, Toyota created transparency to make the process less vulnerable to disruptions. Second, by being less vulnerable to disruptions, Toyota was able to eliminate waste all along the production line, allowing them to keep cost at a competitive level. Accordingly, we first have to create transparency to make our household less vulnerable to guilt, and by doing so, avoid guilt-driven choices. Second, by avoiding guilt-driven choices, we will be able to eliminate wasted energy and time, allowing us to have it all within the course of a 24 hour day, every day.

The logical consequence? To apply the Toyota practice to our household. Sounds a little cold and calculating? Perhaps even a little daunting? But that's exactly why we need to do it: To find out what works, and what could be done smarter.

8

"The Morning Routine"—An Everyday Case Example

Now that we know how great a difference the right process can make, let's see if we can apply the Toyota practice to our household. Let's invite Eiji—of course, in our imagination—to visit a typical American family, just as he visited the Ford assembly line all those years ago and ask him to sit down at their kitchen table and observe their weekday morning routine: What they do, how they do it, and who does what? And then, have him show us how this routine could be executed smarter, the Toyota way.

First, let's meet our imaginary family. There are mom and dad. Both have paid full-time jobs with similar earnings (one year mom's annual salary may be a little higher, another year it's dad's—depending on their bonuses). Their two daughters are both in primary school. Ask mom and dad if they have it all, they would clearly say "no." But ask them if they

"THE MORNING ROUTINE"—AN EVERYDAY CASE EXAMPLE

want to initiate any major changes in their lives, and they would be reluctant. Both have arranged themselves, simply accommodating their daily frustrations and trying to do their best.

Here is what Eiji observes and overhears from the kitchen table: Every weekday morning there is a big rush for the girls to be at school on time. Actually, mom rarely drops them off at the first bell. Usually, they run into the classroom just as the second bell sounds. The situation is annoying for everyone. The girls would love to have some more time to settle in before class starts. Dad can't stand the hectic shouting and frantic running around in the early morning hours and doesn't understand why they can't get this resolved in the first place. And mom doesn't know whom she should be most upset with: The girls for dawdling instead of getting ready, her husband for being annoyed without being helpful, or herself for not getting this under control.

But she has tried everything she can think of: For a while she would get up earlier in order to get herself ready first. But that didn't really work because she hated to prepare breakfast and dress the girls while wearing her business suit and make-up. It made her feel exhausted before she even stepped into the office. Then she tried preparing everything for the girls the night before. But that didn't make the girls any faster in the morning because they simply had a greater opportunity to argue over what to wear. Finally, she told dad that he would have to make breakfast. But given dad's inexperience in the kitchen that only served to slow things down even more. So in the end, mom still had to step in to make sure everyone was fed before leaving the house. Whatever she tried seemed to make the morning routine worse, not better.

After spending a few mornings with the family, it is clear to Eiji that they had a recurring issue with their morning routine, and he suggests they do the same as he instructed his workers to do when they encountered a problem: to create transparency. So, he sits down with mom and dad and asks them what they really want? He learns that mom wants three things: The girls to be neatly dressed and mentally ready for school; herself to be perfectly dressed and mentally ready for work; and, of course, everybody to be fed. Eiji attempts to determine what exactly she means by "neatly and perfectly" dressed? Hearing this, dad then jumps in adding that from his point of view, all three ladies spend too much time getting dressed, as if school and mom's workplace were beauty contests. Stopping dad politely but firmly, Eiji explains that the purpose of this exercise is to reveal each person's true desires. Therefore, mom (as well as the girls) have the right to spend as much time getting dressed as they need if this is important to them. Encouraged by Eiji's comment, mom explains how being dressed for the occasion (for example, a high level meeting) is important to her, which Eiji fully understands. But he has a harder time applying this to the girls and wonders if maybe mom is unnecessarily imposing her own high standards on them as well? Mom is a little surprised at this but agrees to think about it. Eiji has one more question for mom. He is curious to know if mom cares to drop the girls off at school herself? Mom doesn't seem to understand the question. With a skeptical frown she responds

"THE MORNING ROUTINE"—AN EVERYDAY CASE EXAMPLE

that *somebody* has to drop off the girls. Eiji nods in agreement and decides to save the question for later.

Now it's dad's turn. But before Eiji can ask his first question, dad again raises the topic of how long it takes the ladies to get ready. Eiji kindly asks him to focus on himself and try to share what it is that *he* is looking for. Obviously, he seems annoyed at the situation. So what exactly annoys him, and what is it that he wants instead? After some further probing, dad finally reveals that because he must work longer hours in the evening, he keeps hoping to be able to spend some quality time with the girls in the morning. But somehow dressing seems more important to them than spending time with him. Now mom jumps in. She can't believe her ears. Why has he never said so? Eiji calms her down and explains again that this is the whole purpose of this discussion: To create transparency. Eiji then asks dad one more follow-up question. He is wondering if dad has to be at the office at a fixed hour in the morning or if he has some flexibility? Dad answers that he usually tries to be at the office around 8 a.m. but certainly no later than 8:15 a.m. Eiji writes down this fact, and then asks again: Does dad have any flexibility? Dad looks surprised and explains to Eiji with an impatient undertone that of course he has flexibility—like everyone does. But given his seniority, he is expected to set an example and be at his desk well ahead of "the crowd."

With those honest answers on the table, Eiji decides to move on. He can always come back and dig deeper if necessary. But for now he wants them to compare their needs with what they have today. Dad goes first, claiming that his needs are furthest from today's reality. Mom disagrees, claiming that her needs are equally far from reality, because she never has any privacy in the morning to collect her thoughts and get ready for the day. Expanding on this exchange, Eiji encourages them to lay out their daily morning routines, each from his or her own perspective. Then he will share his own observations.

Mom describes getting up, preparing breakfast, eating breakfast with the girls, then helping them to get ready while getting ready herself so they are all ready to leave the house at the same time. Dad describes getting up at the same time, getting himself ready and then eating breakfast while listening to the craziness of the others. Typically, he leaves the house 15-20 minutes before the ladies allowing him to beat the traffic and be at work on time.

Listening attentively to both accounts, Eiji agrees with their descriptions of their individual routines. Then he asks them to identify the bottleneck—the root cause for their daily rush. Dad goes first again and not surprisingly proposes that the source of their problem is in the complexity and chaos created by the way the ladies get dressed. Eiji has to suppress a smile; then he looks at mom, curious to hear what she will propose. To his pleasant surprise, mom agrees that the girls can probably be dressed more efficiently, but that the main problem is that she and the girls are all getting dressed at the same time. As a result, she is unable to concentrate fully on either one while simultaneously having to dress herself. Recognizing that she is on the right path, Eiji asks her to describe the dressing process in more detail. So mom

"THE MORNING ROUTINE"—AN EVERYDAY CASE EXAMPLE

continues, describing how she, as well as the girls, spend much of their time shouting and running back and forth between the parents' and the girls' bedrooms, making the process extremely hectic. Noticing that dad is nodding in agreement, Eiji concludes that the root cause of the daily rush is that these two routines are occurring simultaneously.

Before discussing potential solutions, Eiji wants to share one more observation of his own. He asks them to make a guess as to who is spending how much time getting ready? They both react with a puzzled look, wondering if he really means in minutes? Eiji nods. This time dad hesitates, not wanting to go first. So after a moment, mom offers her estimations, giving herself a slightly higher time than she assigns to dad, just to be on the safe side. However, she has a hard time breaking this estimate down into how much time she spends on herself, and how much time she spends on each of the girls. Then dad offers his perspective, in which, of course, he spends significantly less time than mom.

When Eiji reveals the true numbers, both are shocked: It is dad who takes longest. Dad immediately protests and argues that this can't be true. But when Eiji goes through the details, it begins to make sense. Much of mom's time is wasted by running back and forth between the rooms, by redressing the girls if they get it wrong simply because she can't be with them all the time, and by yelling at dad when he becomes annoyed.

Having thus created full transparency, they are now ready to move on and explore the solution, which presents itself almost automatically. Mom suggests that she could get the girls ready first, and by fully concentrating on them, make sure they stick to their choices and hence get ready faster, much faster indeed. Eventually, she could even go back to the old routine and make them choose their next day's attire the night before. Then dad jumps in and asks how much earlier could they be ready? Mom has a hard time giving him a specific time. But dad is on to something: If the girls are ready early enough, *he* could bring them to school. School is on his way to work anyway. Now mom gets excited too because that would give her full privacy to get ready for work once the others have left the house. Mom and dad look at each other. Could it really be that easy? Eiji understands their astonishment, but isn't surprised. This is what happens when you create transparency.

Now it is mom and dad who have a question for Eiji. Maybe he can tell them why haven't they ever come up with this on their own before now? It seems so simple. Having anticipated this question, Eiji smiles. Leaning back, he looks at mom, then at dad, and explains that they haven't come up with this solution because they couldn't *see* it. Mom and dad are confused. How they could have possibly missed a solution that is so obvious? This time Eiji doesn't answer. Rather, he asks them if they remember how they came up with their old morning routine in the first place? Mom and dad look at each other and shrug their shoulders. They can't really remember, it just somehow evolved. Mom always assumed that she was the one with the more flexible office hours. That's how she ended up dropping off the girls. And dad always assumed that he was less connected with the girls, that the girls would

"THE MORNING ROUTINE"—AN EVERYDAY CASE EXAMPLE

prefer mom. And that's how he ended up allowing mom to take charge.

Eiji frowns and gives mom and dad a skeptical look: Are they really sure that these are the true reasons? And if so, why didn't they simply talk about their assumptions? If they had, they would have easily seen this solution: Dad would have told mom that he does have some flexibility at work. And mom would have told dad that the girls want time with him as much as they want time with her. Done.

Considering the simplicity of the solution, mom and dad are impressed. Eiji is right: They could have come up with this solution themselves *if* they would have kept the lines of communication open and discussed what was troubling them. The question is not how they could have missed the solution, but rather why they didn't have a frank, open conversation? They look at Eiji. How could they have allowed things to reach such a state?

Eiji smiles. He is happy to share his perspective with them, but on one condition: They don't interrupt his explanation until he is finished. Both nod in agreement.

He begins by explaining how mom made herself believe that her schedule was more flexible than dad's simply because it allowed her to do the drop-offs without ever questioning if dad might drop them off, too. Why did she do that? Because prioritizing her work needs over her girls made her feel guilty. What would the other moms think of her? Eiji pauses for a second, then he turns to dad who made himself believe that because mom was the caregiver, the girls were more comfortable with her which, in turn, allowed him to be at the office at 8 a.m. Why did he do that? Because he didn't want to feel guilty for prioritizing the girls needs over the demands of his work. What would his peers think of him?

After another short pause, Eiji turns back to mom. He wonders if she remembers her answer when he asked her earlier whether or not she cares to drop off the girls at school herself? Mom remembers the question, but doesn't recall her answer. Eiji helps her, telling her that she didn't really answer the question. Then Eiji asks dad if he remembers his answer when Eiji asked him if he has any flexibility at work? Dad has the same reaction as mom: He remembers the question, but nothing particular about his answer. Again, Eiji helps by telling him that initially he didn't really answer the question until Eiji insisted. Looking at both of them, Eiji asks them what they feel this says about them? But clearly from their expressions, they have no clue. So Eiji answers the question for them: Mom and dad unconsciously avoided looking at any solution that might trigger guilt. And this, in turn, prevented them from having the kind of conversation that would have led to a mutually acceptable solution like the one they came up with today.

Mom and dad exchange a quiet look. It does sound reasonable to them. But what caused them to change their minds? Why suddenly were they able to accept solutions that previously would have triggered guilt? What had Eiji done to them? Eiji smiles. It was the Toyota method—*his* method—that did the trick: To create transparency, to put their real needs on the table. By forcing mom and dad to honestly confront their true needs, they temporarily found

"THE MORNING ROUTINE"—AN EVERYDAY CASE EXAMPLE

themselves in a guilt-free state of mind, which enabled them for the very first time to see the full solution space. And once they saw the potential benefits concretely laid out in front of them, it was hard to ignore them.

Eiji's words make sense. And the most astonishing thing is that neither mom nor dad feels that they made any sort of unacceptable compromise or trade-off. On the contrary, mom will still be able to see the other moms every day at school during pick up but will now also have the privacy in the morning that she was longing for. And dad will still be at the office by 8:30 a.m. but will now also spend the quality time with the girls he was looking for.

Then, after a short moment of silence, mom adds that she can always step in should dad need to be at the office early. This causes dad to suggest that perhaps he should give making breakfast another try—that is, if mom would teach him. After all, how difficult can it be? Eiji smiles. Now he knows that they are on the right track to tackle the rest of routines on their own. They have learned the most important lesson: By creating full transparency—one routine at a time—they will be able to discover each new solution space that had once been hidden behind their guilt.

9

Learning To See the Obvious

"Do you have a minute, Tom?"

John enters Tom's office after a short knock on his open door. It's Friday and they are both dressed "business casual." Tom gets up and offers John a chair at the conference table in his office:

"Absolutely. I don't have to leave for an hour—until then I'm all yours. What can I do for you?"

"A client meeting…?"

"No, otherwise I wouldn't be dressed like this. I have a parent-teacher conference."

"I see. Everything okay with your kids?"

"They're fine, thanks for asking. The youngest is actually doing great. He wants to sign up for an exchange program. That's what the conference is about…"

"Congratulations. You must be proud."

"Thanks, I am… My daughter, on the other hand…" He

throws John an exasperated grin. "She's just finished high school and is headed for junior college in the fall. I've been trying to advise her on what to study... not that she's listening."

"Been there, done that. Anything school related was always much harder with the girl than with the boy. They somehow tick differently... Anyway, talking about 'gender differences'..." John hesitates. "I'm not even sure what the politically correct term is anymore..."

"You know my opinion about political correctness. Just say what's on your mind."

"What do you think of those initiatives? It's so hard for me to judge. Of course, I want to hire the best women we can find. We need them. But we also need them to become productive contributors to our bottom line... And what about those men talking about a more flexible work schedule, even taking maternity leaves... What's your take? Is there a real need out there? Or is this just another passing fad?"

"Actually, I do think there is a real need, John, but we don't understand it yet. At least I don't. It's very diffuse... and it lacks focus. The truth is, I think it's more of a general desire than an actual movement."

"What do you mean? Do you talk to them about it? I know you've always been much better informed about things like this than I am..."

"I've tried. Remember those three fantastic guys who left last year, one after the other—bum, bum, bum? It really pissed me off. It was such a critical moment in the project, and I lost them all. In any case, I took each one of them out for dinner right before they left. I wanted to understand what's going on—and, of course, try to convince them to stay."

"So?"

"They all kept talking about finding a balance between work and life—or words to that effect. But when I tried to press them on it, ask what they really meant by it, there was never anything concrete. It was a lot about how they wanted to support their wives, how they wanted to spend more quality time with their kids. But there was no real plan. They all had found full time jobs—they were top men—but at companies that promised a more flexible schedule and fewer hours than we were demanding here."

"Combined with a pay cut I assume?"

"In most cases, but that didn't seem to really bother them. Their wives are all working and bringing in decent money, so that wasn't the main driver. Obviously, they do tick a little differently than we used to when we started, John. They definitely do."

"But how much is pressure from their spouses, and how much do they really want it themselves?"

"Good question. I don't know. But I never had the impression that they are doing it for anybody but themselves... But you might want to double-check with Pat. She seems to have a good antenna for those type of topics, without being overly dramatic."

"Will do... interesting. Tell me, Tom, do you really believe we can pull this off—less hours on average with no loss of productivity?"

LEARNING TO SEE THE OBVIOUS

"Yes, John, trust me."

"You know I trust you."

"But it will require some fancy footwork… and there will be some casualties along the way."

"Like what?"

"Having to painstakingly create transparency right down to the bones, every one of us. And then learn how to improve. Not everybody will like it, hence the casualties."

"I can live with that. As long as you don't kill off my top performers… How about stuff like maternity leave?"

"You mean for men?"

"Right."

"I don't see a problem with it; it's all a question of planning."

"But we'll need a cap."

"Why? That's exactly the point. We hire smart people. They don't need to be told what to do to make it work. They can judge for themselves how long they can afford to stay away. And really, the only difference is the duration of the promotion cycle. If you stay away for one year, if you're good enough, you'll be elected Partner in six instead of five years, maybe seven, if you need extra time to build a new client base."

"Hmmm…" John rolls this new idea around in his mind. "This could actually be quite interesting for us, Tom. Think about it… Every time somebody comes back from maternity leave, they have to build a new client base—because their old one has been taken over by somebody else. And these guys are highly motivated. Imagine after so many dirty diapers how much of a relief it will be to sit in Business Class again and watch a movie. This might actually be a new way to broaden our client portfolio."

"John, I'm convinced the biggest beneficiaries of this kind of change will not be our wives, or our kids. It's going to be us."

John stands up, looks at Tom with a smile and gives him a hard pat on his shoulder:

"You've sold me. It looks like a smart move, buddy. I think you may just have done it again…"

He turns to leave, then stops and turns back. "What about this Sherry? She is really impressive… and pretty… "

"No argument from me. She is definitely impressive… and pretty."

"Let me know once you have come up with a concrete plan. I want us to move on it as soon as we can."

Once Tom is in the cab to the parent-teacher conference, he texts Sherry:

"John just stopped by my office. He is fully onboard. We're good to go. Exciting!—When can I hear your voice?"

One of the extraordinary changes Eiji Toyoda brought to production was his ability to identify and eliminate waste. And in retrospect, what he was able to accomplish was not that complicated. In fact, it seems rather intuitive… once we learn how to do it. It will actually feel so right, that once we have embarked on the journey and look back, we will shake our head in disbelief at how much time and energy we used to waste. Even worse, in hindsight, some of the things we used to accept as standard procedure will make us feel embarrassed.

The biggest and most important step comes right at the beginning of the process: To put everything on the table, to create true transparency. If something is not fully disclosed, the process will not work. The key is to ask the right questions (and, of course, not to cheat when answering them). The three critical questions are:[1]

1. "What do I really want?" (Expose our true needs)
2. "What am I doing instead?" (Map out reality)
3. "How bad is it? Or conversely: How much is there room for improvement?" (Put numbers on it)

This is exactly what Eiji did when confronting mom and dad. First, he teased out from each of them what it was that they really wanted without accepting any guilt-driven modesty or pride. Achieving this may require some serious probing in order to get the truth and nothing but the truth on the table. Not because anyone is trying to cheat, but because we simply have been unwilling to confront one critical thing: Our guilt.

Remember the assembly line worker in Detroit who quickly put the defective piece in the storage area behind him to avoid disrupting the production line? It's that same avoidance mechanism. However, creating transparency means just the opposite. It means stopping the production line and not restarting it until you have the truth on the table. This was Eiji's starting point.

Second, Eiji laid out what happens in reality in order to

expose the root cause of the problem, and—equally important—made mom and dad agree on it. We need full agreement on what is really happening today and why before we can discuss how to improve doing things tomorrow. Otherwise we run the risk of making things worse, not better.

Third, Eiji didn't shy away from putting numbers behind each task by mapping out reality, minute by minute—like a protocol. This might sound painful, but it is crucial. As the saying goes: "What you can't measure, you can't improve." Because unless we make the effort to measure each task, we can never be certain we are both talking about the same thing. Equally important, forcing ourselves to put numbers behind every task will cause us to agree on a baseline. And unless we can agree on a baseline, we have no way of knowing whether a task improves, remains the same or perhaps gets even worse. But in order to be able to define the baseline, we first must be able to measure it.

As we begin this process, we obviously have no idea how much time we spend on a given task, nor do we have a sense how much time we *should* be spending on it—if any time at all. Until now, all we cared about was minimizing guilt. But going forward, we *will* care how much time we spend on each task, and by whom the task should be executed. That's why we need the numbers.

Once we have answered all three questions, we will have created full transparency:

LEARNING TO SEE THE OBVIOUS

1. We will know our *true* needs and desires, allowing us to see options that were previously invisible because of guilt.
2. We will know the root cause of the problem, and agree on it together, paving the way for a *joint* solution.
3. We will know the facts. By knowing who spends how much time on what, we will be able to provide a baseline for *conscious* decision making as to how best to allocate our time, rather than relying on our guilt-driven intuition.

"Thank you again for doing this, Arjun. This means a lot to the firm!"

John is going around to each member of the team after the kick-off meeting of the pilot program "Learning to See" while they are packing up. Arjun has to catch a plane; the rest are going out for dinner later in the evening:

"My pleasure, John. As you know, Tom and I have been pushing towards this moment for quite a while. And I think he and Sherry have found exactly the right motivation for our firm to finally move on it."

"I couldn't agree more. Until today when you and Tom explained the Toyota way of working and showed how it could be applied to our business model, I never understood how much time and energy we were wasting. I can't imagine how frustrating it must have been for you and Tom to have to stand by and observe what we were doing knowing there was a better way."

"Oh man, yes. Don't get me started."

"Is your wife okay with your temporary relocation to Chicago?"

"Absolutely. We are one of the traditional families. My wife is taking care of the kids and home and is used to me being on the road." He smiles self-consciously. "But let me tell you, we compensate on the weekends."

"I'm sure you do... Let me know if there is anything I can help you with. And make sure you reach out to me directly. This pilot study is important to me."

"Thank you, John. Will do."

Before rushing to catch his plane, Arjun walks over to Sherry:

"I just wanted to reiterate how excited I am about working with you..." Then with a grin, he adds, "Or should I say 'hunting' with you?"

"Hunting down waste takes a sharp eye and a willingness to make the tough calls. That's why I wanted you with me on the ground in Chicago."

"Thanks. I'll do my best to live up to your expectations. But it's going to be crucial for us to get off to a smooth start. Let's see how fast we can get people going. Given who is on our team, I expect us to move quickly, but you never know."

"Actually, I hope to see some initial improvements in the first month. That would be very exciting!"

"Entirely possible. But it will probably take a couple of months before we see the real benefits. Once we have identified the major 'waste buckets,' it is going to take some serious trial and error before we get things right."

LEARNING TO SEE THE OBVIOUS

"Well, I am ready."

"Me too. See you Monday!"

In the meantime, John has moved on to Valerie. He has never seen her so natural, almost relaxed:

"Excited?"

"Yes, and curious."

"Believe me, so am I. But I fully trust Tom. He has never let me down."

"Oh, I have no doubts that this will work. I'm just curious about the size of the impact. I have been working on this topic for quite a while, but progress has always remained so slow…"

"Must not have been easy, Val… and I didn't help."

"No, you didn't. But at least you were always honest about it."

"Which makes it even more exciting now that we are *both* on board."

"I completely agree. Now if you'll excuse me. I need to catch Sherry before she leaves. See you at dinner, John."

With a smile, Valerie quickly crosses to Sherry for a brief moment alone before they all meet again for dinner. Given their past run-ins, it's an awkward moment for both:

"Hi… I just wanted to say thank you, Sherry."

"Thank me for what?"

"You can't imagine the relief I felt today to finally be working towards a solution rather than fighting one pointless battle after another."

"Actually, I really appreciate you saying that, Val. Because it was your willingness to wage those battles, pointless or not, that made it possible for me to connect with Tom over my frustrations. So while you may have been working on the wrong problem, you still managed to put the topic on everyone's radar in the first place. So thank *you*."

"My pleasure."

"In the end, it's all one big learning process, isn't it?"

"True… I'll let you run."

"See you later."

Before leaving the room, Sherry spots Tom who is now talking with John in the far corner. She winks at him and waves goodbye as she silently mouths the words:

"See you later!"

Waving back, Tom stands as he and John move towards the exit as well:

"Promising kick-off, Tom. I think Arjun and Sherry will turn out to be very effective waste hunters."

"I'll make sure they are."

The moment we create full transparency, waste becomes obvious, painfully obvious. It will appear in two forms: One is pure waste. Pure waste happens when we do something that adds zero value. Pure waste has to be eliminated. Then there is waste from over-engineering. Over-engineering happens when we do something that adds value, but we do it in a more complicated way than necessary. Over-engineered activities can be continued, but they have to be simplified. And by simplifying them, we eliminate the waste. Here are a few "buckets" to look in for waste—activities in today's households that are particularly susceptible waste producers.

LEARNING TO SEE THE OBVIOUS

If we can identify and understand them, they will help guide us in our search for additional waste:

Waste 1—Kids and how we over-indulge them: Sitting on the subway or in a restaurant today, it often feels as if parents have forgotten how to say "no." By virtually agreeing to their children's every demand, parents run the risk of creating unrealistic expectations. Using an extreme example, we find Kids who begin to believe that they are the bosses manipulating their parents by simply threatening to freak out. In such situations, parents are essentially allowing themselves to be held hostage to their children's desires. It is as if parents have become dependent on their kids, not the other way around.

This unfortunate role reversal, for reasons that are manifold, costs us enormous amounts of time (and energy). Think, for example, of the time we waste when offering the child too many choices. The more choices we offer, the more time we waste. For *every* additional choice we offer, we spend additional time: Researching the choice, shopping for the best version of the choice, and waiting for the child to finally choose. The process is maddening: The more choices the child has, the harder it is to choose; and the harder it is to choose, the longer it takes and the higher the probability that the child will change her or his mind at least once. In the process, if the child becomes overwhelmed by too many choices, it falls to the parent to calm and appease the child in order to move on. This holds true for food, clothes, toys, you name it.

The point is, does the child really need and appreciate all

those choices, or is it us as parents attempting to demonstrate that we are "good" parents? Setting aside all the material things, doesn't the child simply want to be fed, dressed, loved, and be left to play in peace? Maybe she or he would even prefer fewer choices and more guidance from us? It's probably safe to say, that most parents could easily eliminate any number of choices that add zero value, and by doing so, significantly simplify the daily selection process—for the child as well as ourselves.

While every household has to define their own standards for how to raise their children, the guiding principle should be to only offer to the child choices that add true value. Think of it as the oil that makes the machine run more smoothly. If you add too little, the machine will work poorly. If you add too much, the machine gets clogged and the overflow must be wiped away. Applying just the right amount will make the machine run efficiently while saving both oil and time. That right amount is what we are looking for. All the rest is waste.[2]

Waste 2—Running a household, and how it is undervalued: Running a household is one of the least appreciated and most misunderstood activities in our lives. And if we really think about it, this is both careless and bizarre given that the whole family depends on it. At its core, the household is nothing less than a microcosm of a factory, a factory that provides a whole range of services to the family who owns and runs it. Without it, no one of the family would be fed, or dressed, or have a clean home to live in. Now you say: But to run this "services" factory, we need money. True. However, the reverse is equally true: To make money, you need the full support of the services factory as well. Nobody is interested in hiring unfed and undressed people who have no home. Bottom line: We need both. But ironically we don't behave like we need both. And that's where we will find hidden waste.

Of course, no one needs a PhD to run a household. But the household can be run in many different ways: Smart ways and foolish ways, time-consuming ways and less time-consuming ways. Somebody has to decide how to run this services factory and make sure it runs smoothly. Similar to all factories, people must be trained in the proper way to do the tasks required. There have to be standards applied that people adhere to, and ideally, there must be regular innovation in order to stay competitive. This used to be the responsibility of the housewife: Mom used to train her daughter/s, and the rest of the family would follow the standards set down by mom (for example, rules pertaining to cleanliness or cooking, etc.). At the same time, housewives used to inspire other housewives to continuously come up with smarter more efficient ways to run their households.

Today, this role has pretty much disappeared and has never been replaced. As a consequence, households are not run anymore, they happen—without training, without standards, without innovation—wasting valuable time and energy along the way. Think for example of mom, who still shoulders the majority of the basic household chores due to her legacy as caregiver, first cleaning up the kitchen after having put the baby to sleep, then folding the laundry, etc. Meanwhile, dad is watching the news and waiting for her to finish. If she instead would simply teach one of these two tasks to dad (or any other able member of the household), they could perform them in parallel and thereby have some joint quality time afterwards.

This idea is often challenged by the fact that mom and dad have different standards, for example with respect to cleanliness. But dad has no problem sticking to standards at his paid work, so neither should he at home. And mom has no problems softening her standards at her paid work, so neither should she at home. We must not allow presumably different standards to become an excuse for waste. Of course, if the standards happen to be insurmountably different, then we probably should let them be and stop complaining.

Finally, dad could inspire mom to do things more efficiently (for example rearranging the kitchen supplies to make the cleaning process faster), and mom could inspire dad to do things smarter (once he has taken over some of the tasks). After all, this is a mutually owned services factory—a household with joint responsibilities towards sharing in both its operational duties and its successes. But until and unless we recognize this, we will keep wasting time with continuous improvisations and daily firefighting.

Waste 3—Work and how we measure success: Today's discussion about the work-life balance is wrong for one simple reason: We are measuring the wrong thing. The whole discussion is focused on how much time we spend at work, not how much work we get done. This fails to do justice to both the employee and the employer. For example, the employee may get work done outside of paid time (think of solving a tricky problem with a clear mind on a Sunday morning), which is technically working for free. And the employer is paying for time that the employee is wasting on non-value adding activities during paid time (think of waiting for input, reading irrelevant email, etc.), which is technically the equivalent of paid vacation time.

The reason why we continue to use time instead of output to measure productivity is partly legacy and partly laziness. Simply put, it's the easiest way to measure it. But working within a prescribed schedule—be it from nine-to-five or nine-to-eight, whether established by policy or by unwritten rules—does not guarantee optimum output. Hence, to maximize their employees' productivity within those predefined hours, most companies create a complex mix of controlling policies and motivating incentive schemes.

Now consider what would happen if we changed the measure of productivity from time to output? The most obvious benefit would be that people could work whenever they wished as long as they accomplished what was required of them. Suddenly, people would start thinking twice before participating in a meeting that only marginally impacts their work. Suddenly, people would start educating their colleagues as to when and when not to copy them on email. Suddenly, time would become valuable because every minute spent on an unnecessary task would be perceived as wasted.

Today, forward thinking companies, such as Netflix and Virgin—both market leaders in their respective industries—are experimenting with changing the way they measure productivity by replacing their traditional holiday policy with a "no policy." They offer their salaried employees the opportunity to take as much time off as they like and whenever they want, as long as the work is done and no other work is hindered, which, de facto, means they are offering the most flexible work arrangement possible.[3]

The moment we change the measure from time to output, the whole notion of part-time versus full-time becomes obsolete. Of course, companies might still decide to institute overlapping work hours in order to provide "face time" for meetings—but everyone interested in optimizing performance will take the initiative and make sure to have overlapping work hours anyway.

In the end, every company has to decide how they want to organize themselves. If a company expects nine-to-eight face time and therefore prefers to exclusively hire people without families or with a stay-at-home spouse, that's a legitimate choice. If in so doing, however, they exhaust the talent pool, they will automatically be forced to adjust their system. The point is, that as long as we keep measuring work by time rather than output, we will keep wasting valuable time while perpetuating a system that was never meant to provide a work-life balance… ever.

"I keep wondering how you do it, Sherry."

Sherry had left after breakfast and was heading home for the weekend. Tom is trying to work from home, but he can't seem to concentrate. Instead, he brings up his favorite Sinatra disc in his Bose Wave Sound Touch and tries to keep himself

LEARNING TO SEE THE OBVIOUS

occupied while he waits for Sherry to land and be back on SMS. He is already missing her. Finally, she connects:

"Landed. How I do *what*?"

"Make me want you... "

"I think this is a question for you, not for me."

"After last night, I want you even more..."

"Do you want me to feel pity for you, Tom?"

"No, thank you, Sherry. I am very happy."

"Good... that's what I thought."

"Don't play it so cool, Madame. You enjoyed it, too!"

"Of course, I did!"

"What did you enjoy most?"

"You want a ranking?"

"As you wish."

"I enjoyed everything... really... just to spend the night with you."

"No, no, Sherry, you need to be more concrete."

"Like what?"

"Like what you enjoyed most?"

"I told you, Tom, everything... every minute... it was beautiful!"

"Now you're trying to be romantic!"

"I am romantic."

"Fine, but I asked a specific question and I want my answer... Usually, you don't make me wait so long... sometimes I even get answers from you without having asked a question!"

"All right, you really want to know what I enjoyed most?"

"Yes."

"Let me think."

"Take your time."

"But then I also want to know what you enjoyed most."

"Sure. Turn-about's fair play."

A minute passes, then two. Becoming impatient, Tom texts her again.

"So…?"

Enjoying this, Sherry decides to tease him.

"Your patience."

"My what…?!"

She laughs, then types:

"Your intensity."

"My intensity doing what, Sherry?"

"Anything… everything you do. Your passion… your desire… It was beautiful."

"Come on, Sherry, stop stalling. How difficult can it be to tell me what you enjoyed most?"

"Why do you need to know anyway?"

"Because I want to take you to heaven."

"You did take me to heaven."

"How often?"

"Excuse me?"

"How often did I take you to heaven?"

"Tom… Is this an interrogation?"

"No, Sherry, no. Think of it as me interviewing a beautiful candidate—but this time I won't refuse to vote…"

"Now you make me laugh, Tom!"

"Don't think you can distract me, Sherry, I'm still waiting for my answer."

LEARNING TO SEE THE OBVIOUS

"I know."

"Let me help you. Do you know what you liked most?"

"Yes… yes, I do."

"But what…? You know what you like, but you're not used to having to talk about it…?"

"Exactly."

"That's all right then, as long as I know you enjoyed it as much as I did."

"Couldn't you see that?"

"Yes, I could, my dear. Your eyes were radiating, your cheeks were glowing… But there might be times when you want something else, something more… And I want to know because I want to give whatever makes you happy… And how can I know if you won't tell me?"

"You are sweet, Tom."

"Not sweet, Sherry. Selfish: The only way I can be happy is if I make you happy… So expect me to keep asking. Because I intend on making absolutely sure you are happy—always."

"I see. Well, I guess I'd better learn to answer your questions then."

"For your own benefit, Sherry."

"For *our* benefit, Tom."

"Yes, my dear… There is only one question you will not be able to answer."

"Which is…?"

"How you do it?"

Once we start creating transparency and we begin to spot waste all around us, what then? The answer is simple: It is the time to develop new more efficient routines to replace the old wasteful ones. Think of routines as micro processes that ensure the smooth functioning of our household, of our services factory. Hence we want them to be as waste free as possible. To achieve that, we have to carefully reassess each one of them. Start small. Pick one routine—for example, the daily morning routine or the weekly shopping routine. Break it apart into its individual tasks, find the waste, come up with a better way, then put the whole routine back together and start implementing the changes. Experiment. One change can often lead to others. The goal is to identify the most effective routine and stick with it.

The simplest way to reduce waste is, of course, to eliminate routines that don't add value to our household, that don't improve our well-being. All other routines—the vast majority of routines—need to be reviewed with an eye towards how they can be simplified or improved, or both. For every routine, we have two means of leveraging a more satisfactory outcome: People (Who should do it?) and tasks (How should it be done?). Let's start with the people—us.

For most tasks we now have two people instead of one available to execute it, which means that the solution space has basically doubled with respect to available time, talent, skills, and ideas. To optimize the efficiency of each routine, we will have to match the right task with the right skill-set at the right time of the day, week or month. Since guilt is no longer the decision driver of who does what, some tasks, even entire routines, will now be executed by our spouse instead of us—or the other way around—and hence might be executed

LEARNING TO SEE THE OBVIOUS

at a different time of day, at a different frequency, and in a different way than they once were.

For particularly repetitive or tiresome tasks, we might want to rotate the task, otherwise nobody will want to do them. We don't want one spouse happily cleaning up the kitchen every night, humming to some Oldies station on the radio and sipping a glass of wine while the other spouse is kneeling on the hard tiled bathroom floor, fighting with the two little ones to get them bathed and ready for bed. In general, the more tasks both spouses can execute, the more flexible and efficient our household becomes, because we can help and replace each other as needed. For example, either can react to unforeseen events such as school closing due to bad weather or a sick child and equally solve the problem.

Let's move on to the tasks. Each routine can now be divided up in many more different ways than they used to be, because we can allocate the individual tasks across the traditional roles and because we no longer have to contend with guilt-driven social control. The challenge is being able to define the best way to execute each routine to satisfy the specific needs of our household (which obviously will differ from household to household). At the beginning, this might require some trial and error experimentation while both are getting used to the new routine. Be creative. Don't try to come up with anything extraordinary or complicated. After all, the whole purpose is to simplify and streamline our daily routines to make our lives easier. Also expect to have to learn some new skills – either because you took over a task you have never done before, or because you decided to do a certain task in a new, smarter way. Last but not least, don't make promises that you won't be able to stick to. These are not New Year's resolutions. These are things you will have to do daily, or weekly. And because they are essential to our daily lives, we want to accomplish them by expending a minimum amount of time and stress.

The thing that will make or break a new routine is fairness. How is the solution perceived by both parents? And by fair, I don't mean a perfectly equal allocation of tasks. Rather—taking everything into account, paid and unpaid work—there must be a sense of equal sharing by both parties so that neither feels unduly put upon. This is something that each household has to define for itself, depending on how they choose to allocate the sum of their responsibilities.

Once we have established the first workable routine, we can add a second one, and a third and so forth. The more routines we add, the more people we touch. Don't expect all of them to be enthusiastic about these changes. Remember discussing the supporters, the resisters, and the large number in-between—the undecided ones? They all will cross our path at one point or the other, be it at work, within the extended family, at school, or within our broader circle of friends. Therefore, it's helpful to anticipate how each might react and how those reactions might impact us.[4]

Let's start with the supporters. They have fully bought into the process and will be with us every step of the way as we replace one outmoded routine after another with a new more efficient one, until we have it all. Their enthusiasm will help inspire us. And should a new routine not work out immediately, we can rely on them to support us and help motivate the more reluctant people around us. However, we should also be aware that even supporters can become a liability if they are overly eager or have unrealistic expectations.

Then there are the resisters. They have fundamental objections to the introduction of new routines and hence will be unsupportive from the start. This is not to say that some of them might turn into supporters once they fully understand the purpose and benefits of the new routines. But the majority of them should be simply ignored. It's a waste of time to argue against somebody who strongly believes in the differences between men and women and their respective roles in society.

Finally, there are the undecided ones on whom it's well worth spending time because they are the ones who eventually will make the difference. There are two types: The first are undecided because they don't have the strength to introduce a new routine on their own. In spite of this, they are desperate to be rescued. They are the ones who have been quietly doing all the work in the background. In the workplace, for example, these are the ones who make sure that everybody has a copy of the document for the meeting even though it's not their job simply because they know how much everybody depends on it. And at home, they are the ones who make sure that all the lights are turned off before going to bed even though they didn't turn them on because they know that if they don't do it, no one will. Their problem is that if they see something amiss, they automatically feel compelled to step in and fix it. Though well-intentioned, this group also presents a danger: Since any new routine will require some experimentation before it runs smoothly, should some undecided but well-intentioned soul continue to step in and prop up the old routine, the new routine will never establish itself. That's why we need to help them understand what we are attempting to accomplish. Luckily, this type of person tends to be very loyal, so it's well worth the investment of time to help bring them along.

The other type of undecided individual simply sees no sense of urgency. They have created an acceptable pattern of behavior for themselves, and before changing anything, they want to be sure the new way works. They leave the experimenting to the others. There is not much we can do about them, except keep them in the loop and, from time to time, share what it is we are doing. Over time, if they see more and more undecided ones turning into supporters, they, too, will come along. Basically, they are late adopters, and the earlier they adopt, the sooner the new majority will take shape.

So, how do we recognize who is with us, actively interested in effecting positive change, who is undecided, and who is against us? Start with our core family unit—our spouse and our self. How do we recognize where each of us stand? By the stories we tell. Resisters and undecided ones will continue to tell the stories we all know too well: "He just doesn't get how to load the dishwasher. My mother was right, men are un-trainable!" or "My wife wants me to spend more quality time with the kids, but it's simply not possible with my job. No matter how many times I explain it, she just doesn't *want* to understand." Both stories indicate that there is a problem. But rather than offering a solution, the storyteller finger-points: It's always somebody else's problem. By shifting the blame, they simultaneously place the burden of solving the problem on the other person's shoulder as well. In the first story, it's the husband who's at fault. In the second story, it's the wife and the employer. In both cases, the storytellers fail to look to themselves as the source of the difficulty and therefore have no chance of identifying a solution.

Supporters' stories will sound completely different: Story one will either sound like "Since my hubby started loading the dishwasher, we have to run it less frequently—no clue how he does it." or "We've decided that I should keep loading the dishwasher but to be fair, he is now cleaning the kitchen stove in the meantime." And story two will either sound like "I don't need more quality time with my kids since I have organized my weekends around them—works better for everyone." or "Since I want to spend more quality time with my kids, I've worked out a new travel schedule with my boss."

What's the difference? There is no finger-pointing and no outsourcing of the problem-solving to others. And no sense of having given up on finding a resolution. On the contrary, it sounds like the storyteller is in the driver's seat, has made a proactive decision, and come up with a plan. Even the tone feels different. Imagine the sense of accomplishment when, for the first time, we realize and eliminate waste, pure waste.

Imagine the excitement when, for the first time, the kids are ready for school 30 minutes ahead of schedule—without any shouting and screaming. And finally imagine the unmistakable sense of having things under control again, and the pride that comes with it when you share the story with others.

And not only will we discover who is a supporter, who is a resister, and who is still undecided, but we may actually learn some surprising truths. Because not everybody who says that they care about equality is a supporter, and not everybody who keeps a low profile is a resister. The stories will not lie. Therefore, with a little careful observation, we will begin to grasp a sense of the evolving landscape of working parents around us.

Over time, these stories will continue to evolve as supporters begin to free up time for rewarding and fun activities rather than just reorganizing the chores, the kids, and paid work. Finger pointing for the resisters will start to feel awkward as the burden of proof shifts from "Are you going home already…?" to "What are you doing still at the office…?" And finally, as more and more of the undecided ones recognize the growing new majority and begin to switch sides, finger-pointing will become less and less attractive until in the end there is nobody left to point a finger at. That's when each of us will know—we have it all.

Outlook: The shape of things to come

If we can turn "Tom & Sherry" into reality, things will look quite different a few years from now. And I'm not only talking about the lives of parents, or parents-to-be. It would be shortsighted, even foolish, to believe that the benefits of having it all are limited to them. There is so much more to it. Let me give you a glimpse of how fundamentally things can change for the better—for all of us.

Prediction 1—The fading star of the "24/7ers": If we can turn "Tom & Sherry" into reality, we will observe more and more companies experimenting with working models that emphasize output over time. Their management teams will begin to develop a clear understanding of how much freedom versus how much control makes their employees most productive. Of course, the employees who are available 24/7 will still be in demand—after all, today's work processes depend on them, and even more importantly, our whole value system is built around them. But their star will begin to fade as more and more employees begin exercising their increasing freedom. In fact, being a 24/7er will start raising questions around quality as well as ability: Why does he need more time than others to finish the job? Is his output truly better, or is he compensating for actually being so much slower? It will also generate questions dealing with sociability: Maybe she has no incentive to go home, maybe nobody is waiting for her? Does she have any friends, or is she simply socially awkward? And finally it will begin raising questions regarding one's intentions: Maybe he is trying to cover up for something, or is he collecting brownie points? Why else would he insist on working such long hours? What is his real agenda? Over time, these questions will be asked more formally and become part of the companies' evaluation and feedback systems. Of course, "hard working" and "fully committed" will still be considered must-have qualities, but being available to work 24/7 will have become suspect.

The impact of getting rid of this self-imposed, abusive working philosophy will be life changing. Think of all the health conditions that are related to chronic stress, such as burnout, sleeplessness, or overweight. Society will be significantly healthier once the 24/7ers have ceased to be the lifestyle to which we aspire. And consider all the accidents that occur on our daily commutes. According to insurance studies, the majority of car accidents happen either close to home, in parking lots, or on our daily commutes—in particular during the evening rush hour. So society will also be a whole lot safer once the 24/7ers are no longer in the mix. And speaking of traffic, imagine how much everyone's trip to and from work will be improved by staggering the workday—having some working from 8 a.m. to 4 p.m., some from 9 to 5, and some from 10 to 6. Instead of sitting in traffic, we will be able to spend that time either at work or at home with our family or catching a movie or maybe a ballgame. A much safer, saner, smarter way of life.

Prediction 2—Back to nature: If we can turn "Tom & Sherry" into reality, we will observe the next generation of parents-to-be experimenting with their additional freedom in order to better control their own futures. Their discussions of how to organize themselves will be much more focused, and their decisions as they embark on their joint journeys as parents will be much more conscious. Women will no longer be forced to secretly assume that their lives will just somehow magically work out once they have a baby. And men will no longer secretly assume that the women will somehow handle it all once they have a baby. But the biggest difference will be how they "plan for" the child. One might expect that finding the "right" moment between two equal careers will be more difficult than finding the "right" moment when there was the unofficial assumption that the woman's career would be put on hold. But instead of pushing childbirth off even further, they will actually be able to turn things around. When negotiating their employment contracts fresh out of college, both men and women will ask for flexibility around parenthood that would have been unthinkable a generation earlier.

How will they do this? By offering a completely new value proposition: To have kids earlier again. The average age of first-time mothers in developed nations has been continuously rising since the 1970s, and has hit the 30 year mark in quite a few European countries. In the US, the mean age is 26, but for college-educated women it is 30 as well.[1] Why does having kids earlier matter? For three reasons:

First, because providing and taking a paid parenting leave will be less expensive. If people have kids earlier, leaves will be taken at an earlier stage of their careers, at a point when it is much easier and significantly less expensive to temporarily replace an employee. Two or three years into a career, employees—both men and women—typically don't have responsibilities and decision making power that will make them seem indispensable later on. Equally, the probability that somebody will "snap up" our job or spot for promotion is much lower since at this point in our careers there are an abundance of career paths still open. So the potential damage that taking a parenting leave can have on our career will be minimized.

Second, because parents will return to work with a different motivation. If people have kids earlier, both—mom and dad—can afford to take a leave, and hence no one will return to work following their leave feeling that they have been forced to take a backseat. Rather, both will return from parenting leave reinvigorated and ready to resume their careers full of energy and aspirations. Furthermore, since each will still command a relatively low salary, they will need both incomes to support their young family.

Third, because the workplace will become an integrated part of the household. If people have kids earlier, parents-to-be will have to think ahead as to how they want to organize their household in order to combine both work and family.

Consequently, they will have negotiated an agreement at the beginning of their employment specifically designed around the projected needs of their family. This will not only break down the artificial barriers between home and work, but also make parents more likely to remain loyal employees. The cost of switching jobs and with it, having to renegotiate work arrangements, will be an added inducement to stay.

But the benefits of having kids earlier go far beyond having it all. It is also significantly healthier for moms as well as for kids. The private and public costs of higher risk pregnancies as well as of fertility treatments are enormous, not to mention the mental cost and pressure associated with such treatments as experienced by so many women today. So society will not only be healthier, but also happier once parents recognize the decided advantages of having children earlier again.

Prediction 3—The one pipeline effect: If we can turn "Tom & Sherry" into reality, we will observe the next generation of students exploring all their options as they take advantage of the additional freedom they will now have to choose their course of study. We will see a steep increase of technically talented women studying disciplines formerly reserved for male students such as engineering or computer science. And we will see an increase of socially talented men going after formerly "female" subjects such as nursing and teaching. With the merger of the pink and blue pipelines into one all encompassing pipeline, the job market will become a completely new ballgame, more competitive and more satisfying for everyone involved.

This Brave New World will be comprised of two

dimensions: First, "matchmaking"—matching of the best candidate with the most suitable job—will improve significantly. There will not only be more choice (as women will have become truly equal contenders in the job market), but there will also be better choices. The reason: If people can choose to study what truly excites them, we can expect them to be more satisfied, and later to be more motivated by the jobs they pursue. Hence, they will perform better which, in turn, will make for happier employers as well as happier employees.

Second, the salary structure will change, becoming more balanced. Of course, this will never be completely true in terms of hierarchy. Having more responsibility will still need to be rewarded with a higher salary. But in terms of which job pays which salary, the concept of "equal pay for equal work" will become a reality. At the same time, we will observe two dynamics: Currently well-paying jobs, for example, ones requiring a background in engineering or computer science, will adjust downwards because more talent will be on the market resulting in more competition for these jobs. And as we all know, greater competition typically lowers the price—in this case the price of talent. Concurrently, less well-paying jobs, for example, nursing or teaching, will adjust upwards for the simple reason that these talents will negotiate harder. We can already observe this trend today with men out-earning women in so-called "pink jobs."[2] With more men beginning to pursue careers in these fields at the same time that women stop believing they are

OUTLOOK: THE SHAPE OF THINGS TO COME

to be pre-destined caretakers and therefore start negotiating their salaries, these jobs will adjust upwards as well.

Hopefully by now you have a firm grasp of the kind of real world changes I envision for our future. All of it is possible. But it is up to us.

Acknowledgements

Writing this book was an exciting, at times challenging journey. I'm grateful…

to Marta Karolak and Celeste Fine for having dared to embark with me on the first leg of the journey;

to Surbhee Groover, Laura Gunning, Judit Hegedus, Kaspar Hohler, Shamal Ratnayaka, Jennifer Sturman, and Daniel Trachsler for their continuous feedback and/or encouragement throughout the journey;

to Garner Simmons for carefully guiding me through the last leg of the journey with his thoughtful edits, and to Jena Pincott for helping me find this thoughtful guide;

to Pandora for providing the vital soundtrack of the journey;

to my parents, Leny and Jaap Glas, and my sister Alexandra Glas, for having believed in this journey long before I even knew of it;

and to Reza Shahrbabaki, without whom no journey would be worth embarking, ever.

Notes

Opening: It used to be so easy

1. While much has been said and written about "having it all" in the context of combining household chores, family, and work, it was Anne-Marie Slaughter's article in The Atlantic that caused me to adopt the term. See Anne-Marie Slaughter, "Why Women Still Can't Have It All," *The Atlantic*, June 13, 2012.
2. The concept of leaning into each other's roles, in particular caregivers who "lean into" the breadwinner's role, was introduced by Sheryl Sandberg. See Sheryl Sandberg, *Lean In: Women, Work, And The Will To Lead* (New York: Knopf, 2013). The idea of flipping the roles was first brought to my attention by Liza Mundy. See Liza Mundy, *The Richer Sex: How the New Majority of Female Breadwinners Is Transforming Sex, Love and Family* (New York: Simon & Schuster, 2012).
3. The theory of specialization, arguing that the traditional role allocation is the most efficient way to run a

household, was introduced by Gary Becker. See *Gary S. Becker, A Treatise on the Family: Enlarged Edition* (Cambridge, MA: Harvard University Press, 1993). For a broader discussion of gender specialization in the household see Gosta Esping-Andersen, *The Incomplete Revolution: Adapting to Women's New Roles* (Cambridge, UK: Polity Press, 2010).
4. U.S. Census Bureau, "Table 1: Educational Attainment of the Population 18 Years and Over, by Age, Sex, Race, and Hispanic Origin: 2014," Current Population Survey, Annual Social and Economic Supplement (2014).
5. Suzanne M. Bianchi, "Family Change and Time Allocation in American Families," paper prepared for the Focus on Workplace Flexibility Conference, Washington, D.C., November 29–30, 2010, 6.
6. In order to better understand the evolution of the broad range of labor-saving devices developed and introduced following World War II, one needs only to scroll through any collection of advertisements from the period portraying dutiful yet cheerful American housewives demonstrating innovations like manufacturer General Electric's Toaster Oven, first introduced in 1956. See http://www.ge.com/about-us/history/1946-1956.
7. Private time includes "personal care" (sleeping, eating, grooming) as well as "free time" (time spent on education, religion, organizations, event, visiting, fitness, hobby, TV, reading, stereo, and communication). See Bianchi, "Family Change," 6.

8. Bianchi, "Family Change," 8.
9. While struggling with feelings of guilt as a new mom, I decided to read a few "Mommy Books." What I discovered was that I wasn't alone. In fact, the phenomenon of the guilty mom is widespread. See Rory Freedman and Kim Barnouin, *Skinny Bitch: Bun in the Oven: A Gutsy Guide to Becoming One Hot and Healthy Mother!* (Philadelphia: Running Press, 2008); Ayelet Waldman, *Bad Mother: A Chronicle of Maternal Crimes, Minor Calamities, and Occasional Moments of Grace* (New York: Doubleday, 2009); Stefanie Wilder-Taylor, *Sippy Cups Are Not for Chardonnay and Other Things I Had to Learn As a New Mom* (New York: Simon Spotlight Entertainment, 2006).
10. Bianchi, "Family Change," 8.
11. Wendy Wang, Kim Parker and Paul Taylor, *Breadwinner Moms*, Pew Research Center (May 29, 2013), 12.
12. In terms of actual time spent with their kids, dads tend to devote a disproportionate amount of their time to recreational activities as compared to moms, who spend more time on physical and managerial care (in absolute and relative terms). Recreational activities tend to be fun such as playing catch, or doing arts and crafts, or just talking, etc. However, these activities are neither routine nor vital to a child's basic needs. Physical and managerial activities, on the other hand, are essential to a child's wellbeing. Physical activities include daily, essential activities such as feeding, dressing, personal

hygiene, etc. Managerial activities include tasks like organizing and managing childcare, picking up and dropping off the kids from school or other similar activities. See Sara Raley, Suzanne M. Bianchi, and Wendy Wang, "When Do Fathers Care? Mothers' Economic Contribution and Fathers' Involvement in Child Care," *American Journal of Sociology* 117, no. 5 (2012), 1422-1459.

1. Why Guilt Matters

1. Given the need for a thorough understanding of what guilt is and how it impacts human behavior, I'm indebted to Herant Katchadourian for writing his comprehensive yet accessible book on guilt. See Herant Katchadourian, *Guilt: The Bite of Conscience* (Stanford: Stanford University Press, 2010). For a more theoretical examination of guilt, see Jessica L. Tracy, Richard W. Robins, and June Price Tangey, eds., *The Self-Conscious Emotions: Theory and Research* (New York: The Guilford Press, 2007).
2. Katchadourian, *Guilt*, 3-4, 167-191.
3. The example used here is derived from the one provided in Tracy, Robins, and Tangey, *Self-Conscious Emotions*, 6.
4. Katchadourian, *Guilt*, 7-8, 117-119.
5. Katchadourian, *Guilt*, 21-24, 60-61.
6. Katchadourian, *Guilt*, 15-19, 24-27.

NOTES

2. When What We See Is Not What It Seems

1. This line of thought was inspired by a weekly audio podcast "Arming the Donkeys," produced by Dan Ariely. The specific podcast noted here was devoted to how we make difficult decisions, in particular in situations where there are only undesirable options, options that you wouldn't choose unless you had no other choice. The research presented shows that people in those situations tend to prefer outsourcing the decision to someone else rather than deal with it themselves. See Dan Ariely and Simona Botti, "Making Difficult Decisions," *Arming the Donkeys* (May 21, 2012).
2. In her book "Opting Out? Why Women Really Quit Careers and Head Home", Pamela Stone observes stay-at-home moms "professionalizing their volunteer work" and treating it as a "second career". See Pamela Stone, *Opting Out? Why Women Really Quit Careers and Head Home* (Berkeley: University of California Press, 2007), 173-177.
3. This line of thought is built upon the concept of "social defense" as explored in a paper by Irene Padavic and Robin J. Ely. In it, the authors argue that organizations use the "work-family narrative" (e.g., that women are less successful at work because of the daily conflict between family obligations and long work hours) as a "social defense" to protect their male employees from having to confront the true reasons for spending excessive hours at work. See Irene Padavic and Robin J.

Ely, "The Work-Family Narrative as a Social Defense," paper presented at the "Gender and Work: Challenging Conventional Wisdom" Research Symposium, Harvard Business School, March 1, 2013.
4. In her meta-analysis of dozens of studies (i.e., a statistical method in which the data of several separate but similar studies are pooled to test for their statistical significance), Janet Shibley Hyde observes that gender differences have either no or a very small effect on most of the variables examined. Besides motor performance (i.e. how fast and how far we can throw an object), she finds only two additional areas with significant differences: Sex (in particular, how often we masturbate, and how we think about casual sex) and aggression (in particular, physical aggression). See Janet Shibley Hyde, "The Gender Similarities Hypothesis," *American Psychologist* 60, no. 6 (2005), 586.
5. Bureau of Labor Statistics, "Table B-1: Employees on nonfarm payrolls by industry sector and selected industry detail," Establishment Data (June 05, 2015).
6. Sandrine Devillard et al., *Women Matter 2013 – Gender Diversity in Top Management: Moving Corporate Culture, Moving Boundaries*, McKinsey & Company (November 2013), 10-11.
7. In her chapter on mentoring, Sheryl Sandberg uses the analogy of a baby bird looking for its mother (based on a book she loved as a child) to illustrate the meaning and power of mentoring. See Sandberg, *Lean In*, 64-76.

8. In a more recent study, Bobbi J. Carothers and Harry T. Reis, while applying a different methodology, reach the same conclusion as Janet Shibley Hyde, that the similarities between men and women outnumber the differences between them. See Bobbi J. Carothers and Harry T. Reis, "Men and Women Are From Earth: Examining the Latent Structure of Gender," *Journal of Personality and Social Psychology* 104, no. 2 (2012), 385-407. The authors summarize their findings using more accessible language in The New York Times: Bobbi Carothers and Harry Reis, "The Tangle of the Sexes," *The New York Times*, April 20, 2013. Another, more practical perspective (gained from their daily practice as child psychologists specializing in the treatment of boys) is provided by Dan Kindlon and Michael Thompson, who arrive at the same conclusion that "men and women are a lot more the same than they are different." See Dan Kindlon and Michael Thompson, *Raising Cain: Protecting the Emotional Life of Boys* (New York: Ballantine Books, 2009), 13.
9. "Why Swedish Men Take so Much Paternity Leave," *The Economist*, July 22, 2014.
10. For a discussion of similar approaches (and their early "successes") in other countries, see Liza Mundy, "Daddy Track: The Case for Paternity Leave," *The Atlantic*, January/February 2014.
11. Sandrine Devillard et al., *Women Matter 2013*, 15-17.

3. When High Performers Underperform

1. Jeff Denneen, "Let's Fix It: Kill the Weekly Meeting," *LinkedIn*, October 13, 2014; Scott Dockweiler, "How Much Time Do We Spend in Meetings? (Hint: It's Scary)," *the muse*, October 15, 2014; Michael C. Mankins, "This Weekly Meeting Took Up 300,000 Hours a Year," *Harvard Business Review*, April 29, 2014.
2. For "one-of-a-kind imaginative cupcake designs" see The New York Times Best-seller by Karen Tack and Alan Richardson, *Hello, Cupcake!: Irresistibly Playful Creations Anyone Can Make* (Boston: Houghton Mifflin Company, 2008).
3. Linda Babcock and Sara Laschever, *Women Don't Ask: The High Cost of Avoiding Negotiation—and Positive Strategies for Change* (New York: Bantam Dell, 2007), 2.
4. The concept of the "flexibility gap" for men was inspired by a number of articles including Jason Hall, "Why Men Don't Take Paternity Leave," *Forbes*, June 14, 2013, Liza Mundy, "Daddy Track," and Lauren Weber, "Why Dads Don't Take Paternity Leave," *The Wall Street Journal*, June 12, 2013.

4. The Grand Delusion We All Fall For

1. Binyamin Appelbaum, "Disney Turned 'Frozen' Into a Cash Cow," *The New York Times Sunday Magazine*, November 23, 2014.

2. Christina Hoff Sommers, "You can give a boy a doll, but you can't make him play with it," *The Atlantic*, December 6, 2012.

3. A research study conducted by Janice Hassett, Erin Siebert, and Kim Wallen observed and analyzed the ways in which 34 monkeys played with human toys. These toys were categorized as either masculine (wheeled toys such as trucks and cars) or feminine (plush toys such as stuffed animals and dolls). While the male monkeys showed a strong and consistent preference for the wheeled toys, the preferences of the female monkeys were more balanced. However, the male monkeys did play with the plush toys from time to time. Furthermore, the researchers caution against over-interpreting their results, in particular since they can't exclude other factors such as the size or color of the toys that might have influenced the monkey's choices. See Janice M. Hassett, Erin R. Siebert, and Kim Wallen, "Sex Differences in Rhesus Monkey Toy Preferences Parallel Those of Children," *Hormones and Behavior* 54, no. 3 (2008), 359-364.

4. Julia Plevin, "Don't Fear the Male Babysitter," *The Atlantic*, July 19, 2013.

5. For a summary of the latest findings in education by the Organization for Economic Co-operation and Development (OECD), see OECD, *Trends Shaping Education 2015 Spotlight* 7 (Paris: OECD Publishing, 2015). For full reports, see OECD, *PISA 2012 Results:*

What Students Know and Can Do–Student Performance in Mathematics, Reading and Science (Volume I, Revised edition) (Paris: OECD Publishing, 2014); OECD, *Closing the Gender Gap: Act Now* (Paris: OECD Publishing 2012).

6. An often discussed phenomenon in this context is the so-called "stereotype threat," which describes a situation in which women underperform in math when competing against men, but perform normally when competing against women. See Steven J. Spencer, Claude M. Steele, and Diane M. Quinn, "Stereotype Threat and Women's Math Performance," *Journal of Experimental Social Psychology* 35 (1999), 4–28. In a similar vein, the OECD concludes in its latest PISA study (which tested performance in math while simultaneously questioning student attitudes towards math) that girls feel more anxious than boys towards math, and therefore have less confidence in their own math skills, even when they perform equally well. See OECD, *Are Boys and Girls Equally Prepared for Life?* (Paris: OECD Publishing, 2014), 5.
7. OECD, *Trends Shaping Education*, 6.
8. OECD, *Trends Shaping Education*, 7.

5. What We Have in Common with Smokers

1. Rachel Abrams, "CVS Stores Stop Selling All Tobacco Products," *The New York Times*, September 3, 2014; Stav

NOTES

Ziv, "Cigarette Maker To Phase Out Smoking in its Offices," *Newsweek*, October 23, 2014.
2. Centers for Disease Control and Prevention (CDC), "Trends in Current Cigarette Smoking Among High School Students and Adults, United States, 1965–2011," National Health Interview Survey (1965–2011).
3. "The cigarette industry: Running out of puff," *The Economist*, January 25, 2014.
4. According to the Merriam-Webster Online Dictionary, the first known use of the term secondhand smoke was in 1976. See http://www.merriam-webster.com/dictionary/secondhand smoke.
5. "A History of Advocacy," Americans for Nonsmokers' Rights, accessed June 16, 2015, http://www.no-smoke.org/pdf/historyadvocacy.pdf.
6. "State Laws Restricting Smoking by Location," American Lung Association, accessed June 16, 2015, http://www.lungusa2.org/slati/appendixb.php.

6. What We Really Want (But Are Afraid to Ask For)

1. The object here was to explore the ways in which today's moms and dads might allocate their time between work and home if they had a true choice. My analysis and underlying assumptions were as follows: To understand today's allocation, I started with the official employment status data provided by the Bureau of Labor Statistics, "Table 5. Employment status of the population

NOTES

by sex, marital status, and presence, and age of own children under 18, 2012-2013 annual averages." I then obtained the results to two questions taken from surveys conducted by the Pew Research Center that I felt revealed moms' and dads' "ideal situation". The first question was straight forward asking moms and dads with children under 18 years of age what their ideal working situation would be: "Full time", "Part time", or "Not at all". The answers to this question provided a first "snapshot" of the true needs of today's moms and dads. But since the term "part time" is still highly stigmatized, particularly among men, I chose a second question to clarify the picture and thus make certain we are including the true needs of all (even those who might object to using this term). This second question asked moms and dads with children under 18 years if they spend "Too little", "Right amount", or "Too much" time with their children. I used the answer "too little" as an indicator of the true needs of those moms and dads who would prefer some sort of flexible working arrangement that allows them to spend more quality time with the kids, but not necessarily work part time. The results of this survey are presented in Kim Parker and Wendy Wang, *Modern Parenthood: Roles of Moms and Dads Converge as They Balance Work and Family*, Pew Research Center (March 14, 2013), 11-12 for first question, 2-3 for second question. Analyzing the data for moms resulted in the following: In 2012, 70% of moms whose children were under the age of 18 were in the labor force (including those who described themselves as "unemployed") while 30% stayed home. According to the answers to question one from the Pew Research Center, 37% of working moms said working full time would be ideal, 50% preferred part time, and 11% preferred not working at all ("Don't know/Refused" responses were not included). Of the stay-at-home moms, 63% said that either working full time or part time would be ideal, and 36% preferred not working at all. Thus, if we take the 70% of today's working moms and re-allocate them according to their "ideal situation", we have 26% who prefer to work full time, 35% who prefer to work part time, and 8% who prefer to stay home. If we then apply the same methodology to today's 30% stay-at-home moms (and, since we don't have a breakdown for part time versus full time, we can assume a similar breakdown for the working moms), we end up with 9% who prefer to work full time, 10% who prefer to work part time, and 11% who prefer to stay at home. If we combine these figures, we have 35% who prefer to work full time, 45% who prefer to work part time, and 19% of moms who prefer to stay at home. According to the second question, 23% of moms say they spend too little time with their children versus 68% who say they spend the right amount and 8% who say they spend too much. This means that 23% of the 35% (or approximately 8%) of moms who said they prefer to work full time, in fact, prefer a solution that allows them to spend more quality time with their kids than their current job allows. So if we move that 8% from a full time to a part time, respectively, we end up with 27% of moms who prefer to work full time, 53% who prefer some sort of flexibility, and 19% who prefer to stay at home. Analyzing the same data for dads we find that in 2012, 93% of dads whose children were under the age of 18 were in the labor force (including those who self-identified as "unemployed") and 7% stayed home. According to the first question posed by the Pew Research Center, 75% of working dads said working full time would be ideal, 15% preferred part time, and 10% preferred not working at all. We don't have separate data for stay-at-home dads. But that doesn't dilute the analysis, as the vast majority of dads are working dads anyway. Now if we take that 93% of today's working dads and reallocate them according to their "ideal situation," we have 70% who prefer to work full time, 14% who prefer to work part time, and 9% who prefer to stay home. If we combine this with today's 7% stay-at-home dads, we have 70% who prefer to work full time, 14% who prefer to work part time, and 16% of dads who prefer to stay at home. According to the second question, 46% of dads say they spend too little time with their children, versus 50% who say they spend the right amount and 3% who say they spend too much. This means that 46% of the 70% (or approximately 32%) of dads who said they prefer to work full time, in fact would prefer a solution that allows them to spend more quality time with their kids than their current job offers them. So if we move those 32% from a full time to a part time respectively, we end up with 38% of dads who prefer to work full time, 46% who prefer some sort of flexibility, and 16% who prefer to stay at home.

7. If You Want Something, Say So...

1. This tale is built upon the detailed description of the rise and fall of mass production and the emergence of lean production in James P. Womack, Daniel T. Jones, and Daniel Roos, *The Machine That Changed the World* (New York: Free Press, 2007), 19-69.
2. Womack, Jones, and Roos, *The Machine*, 41.
3. Womack, Jones, and Roos, *The Machine*, 42; "U.S. Total Vehicle Sales Market Share by Company, 1961-2012," Ward's Automotive Reports, retrieved October 22, 2013.
4. This and the following quote: Womack, Jones, and Roos, *The Machine*, 77.
5. Womack, Jones, and Roos, *The Machine*, 81.
6. Mona El-Naggar, "In Lieu of Money, Toyota Donates Efficiency to New York Charity," *The New York Times*, July 26, 2013.

9. Learning to See the Obvious

1. The approach proposed in this chapter is derived from John Drew, Blair McCallum, and Stefan Roggenhofer,

NOTES

Journey to Lean: Making Operational Change Stick (New York: Palgrave Macmillan, 2004).
2. Drew, McCallum, and Roggenhofer, *Journey to Lean*, 116.
3. Claer Barrett, "Richard Branson tells staff: take as much holiday as you like," *Financial Times*, September 25, 2014; Daniel H Pink, "Netflix lets its staff take as much holiday as they want, whenever they want–and it works," *The Telegraph*, August 14, 2010.
4. Drew, McCallum, and Roggenhofer, *Journey to Lean*, 177.

Outlook: The shape of things to come

1. OECD, "SF2.3: Age of Mothers at Childbirth," OECD Family Database.
2. Shaila Dewan and Robert Gebeloff, "More Men Enter Fields Dominated by Women," *The New York Times*, May 20, 2012.

About the Author

Elisabeth Glas is a trained historian-turned-management consultant with a strong belief in the power of reframing a problem in order to unlock its solution. Born and raised in Switzerland, she divides her time between Manhattan and Milan. *Tom & Sherry* is her debut.

www.ingramcontent.com/pod-product-compliance
Lightning Source LLC
Chambersburg PA
CBHW031346040426
42444CB00005B/206